W9-BCS-145

HUMAN ECOLOGY
AND SUSCEPTIBILITY
TO THE
CHEMICAL ENVIRONMENT

HUMAN ECOLOGY AND SUSCEPTIBILITY TO THE CHEMICAL ENVIRONMENT

Sixth Printing

By

THERON G. RANDOLPH, M.D.

CHARLES C THOMAS · PUBLISHER
Springfield · Illinois · U.S.A.

56677

Published and Distributed Throughout the World by
CHARLES C THOMAS ● PUBLISHER
Bannerstone House
301-327 East Lawrence Avenue, Springfield, Illinois, U.S.A.

© *1962, by* CHARLES C THOMAS ● PUBLISHER
ISBN 0-398-01548-1
Library of Congress Catalog Card Number: 61-15380

First Printing, 1962
Second Printing, 1967
Third Printing, 1970
Fourth Printing, 1972
Fifth Printing, 1976
Sixth Printing, 1978

With THOMAS BOOKS *careful attention is given to all details of
manufacturing and design. It is the Publisher's desire to present books that
are satisfactory as to their physical qualities and artistic possibilities and
appropriate for their particular use.* THOMAS BOOKS *will be true to those
laws of quality that assure a good name and good will.*

Printed in the United States of America
R-1

PREFACE

MOST ILLNESSES were originally thought to have arisen within the body. Only recently has this age-old concept been challenged. [The importance of the outside environment as a cause of sickness was first demonstrated in respect to infectious diseases about eighty years ago and to allergic diseases approximately fifty years ago. Although the general principles of infectious disease are now fully accepted and applied, the medical profession has been slow in learning and applying the necessary techniques to demonstrate cause and effect relationships between the non-microbial environment and ill health.

Since the diagnostic measures necessary to demonstrate causation are rarely employed, physicians all too frequently remain content to treat the effects of illness. This is particularly true of continuous or frequently repeated environmental exposures which are usually not suspected as common causes of chronic ills. Treating the effects of chronic illness not only often fails to provide an adequate medical service, but frequently extends and complicates chronic illnesses so treated.

A wider frame of reference is needed. It is the relationship between man and his environment, including his diet—so-called human ecology—that is of prime importance. Strangely, the basic biologic laws of human ecology have not been adequately stated. Neither has the full range of environmental incitants capable of eliciting clinical responses been fully described.

Of the various physical, biologic and chemical incitants capable of inducing susceptibility and impinging on the health of individuals, the man-made chemical environment is the least understood. Indeed, the totality of this chemical environment and interrelationships between facets of it have not been adequately described. This manuscript is an attempt to fill this void.

[*v*]

This is a clinically oriented presentation. It does not purport to describe the chemical environment in an inclusive manner. Only those chemical exposures that have been incriminated as causes of reactive symptoms are listed. Various other environmental chemicals are not described, for as yet, they have not been demonstrated as causes of clinically detectable reactions—at least in the exposures as ordinarily encountered. Occupational exposures are not considered within the scope of this monograph.

The writer is especially indebted to his patients for making this presentation possible. Without their observations, their intelligent cooperation in submitting to experimentally arranged exposures and their compliance with recommendations, this monograph would not have been possible.

Finally, I wish to acknowledge the support of the Human Ecology Research Foundation in the preparation of the manuscripts upon which this book is based.

T. G. R.

CONTENTS

HUMAN ECOLOGY
AND SUSCEPTIBILITY
TO THE
CHEMICAL ENVIRONMENT

Part I

BACKGROUND

INTRODUCTION

How SAFE is our present chemical environment? To what extent does it contribute to chronic illness? How much do we know about the long-term effects of such by-products of "progress" as the chemical pollutants in the air of our homes and cities; chemical additives and contaminants in our foods, water and biological drugs, as well as our synthetic drugs, cosmetics, and many other personal exposures to and occupational contacts with man-made chemicals?

As new chemicals are constantly being developed for new uses, so-called "safe tolerances" are determined by the results of *animal toxicity studies.* Although checking the response of groups of animals to single substances undoubtedly has protected us from *acute* reactions and reduced *chronic* toxicity in humans, is this enough? Are the results of such chronic toxicity studies to *one specific chemical,* made in *animals* and under ideal laboratory conditions, applicable to *humans* who are daily subjected— often during their lifetime— to *this* chemical and to many *related* chemical exposures? Is not modern man's increasing chemical environment impinging on his health and general welfare?

Since the crux of this problem of man versus man-made chemicals hinges on individual susceptibility and individual adaptation to this environment, several more questions arise. Have animals in the course of these long-term toxicity studies been tested with the excitant under investigation during a phase of adaptation in which reactions on the basis of *individual susceptibility* are accentuated? Or has the occurrence of aberrant responses indicative of individual susceptibility been averaged

[3]

out? These are *important questions* because the medical problem involved here, in respect to individual susceptibility, is *not* concerned with the *middle* of the distribution curve, but with the *far end!* Whereas acute and chronic toxicity studies of new chemicals in animals are indispensible as *preliminary screening processes,* these should be regarded as a *prelude to observations in man*—especially in susceptibility-prone individuals. Where are these reports? The few that exist tend to involve intermittent exposures and to appear some time *after* the production and distribution of a new chemical has become a "profitable venture."

Indeed, some of the most troublesome chemical exposures have not been adequately described and there is no general knowledge of their potential *hazards*. The chief reason for this is that these materials have become integral parts of our current existence. Not being readily avoided accidentally, they are not usually suspected. Not being suspected, they are not usually avoided deliberately. Thus, not being eliminated either by chance or design, certain common chemical exposures remain unsuspected causes of *chronic physical and mental illnesses*. Even though certain chemical exposures may be suspected, avoidance is not only inconvenient and sometimes expensive but, because of the addiction-like responses that may be involved, these exposures often run counter to the desires of certain highly susceptible victims. Thus, observations of individual susceptibility to chemical excitants in humans have been *obstructed* by continuity of exposure and self-perpetuation of the process.

From the material to be presented, it may be said that an *analytical investigation* of the safety of the chemical environment in laboratory animals *has not* answered the above-posed questions. Neither may it be assumed that the observed effects from *controlled* exposures in animals are analagous to the *happenstance* exposures in man. Our analytical investigators seem to have wandered away from the question they set out to solve; the more minutely they have subdivided this problem, the more difficult it is to rejoin its parts. In other words, the sum of the toxicologists' analytical data accruing from animal experiments is *far removed* from the situation confronting humans in their daily lives.

A clinically oriented *synthesis* of the subject is needed. Although a doctor faced by a complaining, chronically sick patient may suspect several chemical exposures, the patient may be reacting to these as well as several *other* unsuspected and related ones. Not knowing the scope of the chemical excitants that might be involved nor how to protect his patient from the potential total of them, the doctor often remains at a loss in handling such a case. Because the totality of the chemical environment and its range of potential clinical effects have not been described, the physician is apt to treat such a patient with *additional* chemically derived drugs, thereby aggravating his problem. Obviously, a broader view and a more fundamentally sound basis of therapy are needed.

Human Ecology

The term *ecology* was first used by Haeckel in 1866 (1) in referring to the mutual relations of organisms to their physical conditions of life and to each other, as described by Darwin (2). Human ecology embodies the concept of a person's adaptation to the conditions of his existence. The ecologic effects of chemical excitants are observed most advantageously by first insulating an individual from the *total chemical environment* and then observing his response to *re-exposure* to previously avoided *parts* of it (3,4). This clinically oriented regimen produces an entirely different set of answers to the above questions than currently is supplied by the toxicologists.

The following preliminary summary of the application of this approach in practice may be made:

Chemical excitants—poisons, irritants and various lesser man-made chemical exposures usually regarded as harmless in the dosages encountered—may induce acute or chronic clinical effects, depending principally on dosage and host susceptibility. On one extreme are the acute immediate reactions from massive exposures which are readily apparent and generally harmful to all. Fortunately, we are largely protected from such acute effects by a general knowledge of their harmfulness. On the other extreme are the chronic symptoms traceable to the long-term subtle impingement of frequently encountered lesser exposures to which an ever-increasing minority are apparently becoming susceptible.

Unfortunately, we are neither adequately protected from these chronic effects nor generally aware of the potentially noxious nature of such everyday chemical exposures.

Since the biological problem resulting from exposure to, susceptibility to, and maladaptation to diverse environmental chemical exposures has not been adequately presented from the standpoint of *an individual buffeted by his chemical environment,* this article will attempt to fill that void. In doing so, the writer will draw heavily on his clinical observations during the past two decades. The scope of the subject precludes biographical completeness. This is not a *review* but the presentation of a *point of view* and the program for a common medical problem, previously not recognized satisfactorily and which, heretofore, the writer has only presented preliminarily (5,6,7,8).

Adaptation

The body responds to the long-term inurement of environmental excitants in a basically similar manner—that is, by adapting to them. Selye (9,10) described the common features and stages of adaptation to a wide range of materials as the *general adaptation syndrome.* Adolph (11) observed similar stages of adaptation, but found that individual animals not only exhibited marked differences in their responses to the same excitant but also that these manifestations tended to overlap and were more often *specific* to one stressor than general to more than one.

A Clinical Observer's View of Adaptation

Despite the importance and general dissemination of Selye's views, the basic biological concepts of adaptation and ecology described by physiologists and other biologists have not been widely applied to the practice of medicine. There seem to be several reasons for this:

1)   Traditionally and in contrast to scientists, with the possible exception of pediatricians, physicians have been more concerned with the treatment of individual patients than with observations of the natural course of illness as exhibited by untreated cases.

2)   Whereas physiologists have described the sequential stages

of adaptation as a I, II, III phenomenon (alarm reaction, stage of resistance, and stage of exhaustion, respectively), most physicians first see their patients toward the latter part of stage II of adaptation.

In the practice of medicine, one does *not* start with young healthy individuals of uniform age and ancestry who have led previously protected lives, exposing them to regular doses of a given material under controlled conditions and *watch them sicken,* as do physiologists and toxicologists in their animal tests. Doctors ordinarily enter upon the scene when an individual patient is already sick, as a result of a relative exhaustion of a long-term interplay between him and given portions of his environment. It is much as if the physician arrived at the theatre sometime during the last scene of the *second* act of a three-act play—puzzled by what may have happened previously to the principal actor, his patient. To what, how long and how effectively such a sick person may have been adapting remain unknown. The important point is that the full significance of his adaptation is apt to be missed *unless* an attempt is made to reconstruct earlier stages.

3) As a clinical observer, the writer agrees with Adolph (11) that the combinations and modifications of adaptation in a given person are specific to the excitant. Although Selye (9,10) recognized this possibility, he placed relatively greater emphasis on the general features of adaptation.

4) Lastly, there has been little medical interest in the patient as a whole and his adaptations as an integrated unit to the outside world. This seems to have been due in part to the progressive fractionation of medical practice into specialty subdivisions as well as to the tendency to investigate medical problems by means of a *fractional analysis* of them.

An attempt to synthesize these discordant views held by academicians and clinical observers led the writer to describe the *specific adaptation syndrome.* Since this concept of a person as a functionally integrated unit responding to his environment has been reported only preliminarily (12), it will be reviewed briefly before describing the chemical environment and its clinical effects.

The Specific Adaptation Syndrome

Stripped of all interpretations as to mechanisms and stated in simplest terms, the specific adaptation syndrome is a *clinical counterpart* of Selye's general adaptation syndrome. It also consists of merging non-adapted, adapted, and non-adapted developmental stages.

Adaptation is so characteristic of life that an individual usually is oblivious of his adaptive responses to various common materials. Being relatively improved immediately after each specific exposure to which he is adapting, a person may resort to it in an addiction-like manner as often as necessary to remain "picked up." Indeed, this may be the only way he knows to postpone or relieve his otherwise inevitable delayed "hangover-like" reactions, for only thereby does he remain "normal" and without complaints. More commonly, however, such an adapted person simply eats what he likes and does what he is accustomed to do as often as desired without the slightest notion of "adapting" or being involved in any addiction-type of response. Only when one or more of his specific adaptive responses taper off and the stage of exhaustion is approached does he start to complain—a change ordinarily regarded by all concerned as the *onset* of the present illness.

But if *chronic cumulative exposures* to an offending substance acting in this manner are avoided, the following tends to occur: 1) "Hangovers," first accentuated, diminish and disappear as adapted or partially adapted stages (II or III) revert to the initial non-adapted stage (I).   2) Re-exposure to an *isolated dose* of such a previously avoided material then induces an immediate acute reaction which   a) *changes chronic illness to acute illness,* and   b) *demonstrates the causation of many chronic syndromes.*

Each subsequent *widely spaced* specific exposure precipitates a similar acute reaction, but with oft-repeated doses, immediate post-exposure effects quickly taper off with the recurrence of a relatively symptom-free, specifically adapted state.

Environmental Factors Eliciting Adapted Responses

Many go through life adapting to various physical, biological and chemical environmental materials without apparent ill effects. But in those who happen to become increasingly susceptible, doses ordinarily taken in stride become pathogenic, frequently inducing degrees of maladaptation associated with chronic illness. This concept that chronic disease syndromes commonly result from frequent exposures to environmental substances to which susceptibility exists is *not* widely appreciated in medicine. Consequently, a brief reference to physical and biological agents inducing adapted and maladapted responses will aid in understanding similar effects attributable to environmental chemicals.

The human race has had millions of years to adjust to cold, light and other solar radiations as well as various other physical exposures. As a consequence, only a few current specimens become sufficiently susceptible and maladapted to manifest symptoms of so-called *physical allergy.* Likewise, most of us are adequately adapted to common foods, plant pollens and oils, spores, insects and other animals. But some become increasingly susceptible to one or more of these common materials and some of this group become chronically sick as a result of *decreasing adaptation* thereto. Similar effects attributable to susceptibility to common chemical exposures currently are not appreciated as major causes of chronic illness. In fact, neither the chemical excitants nor the full range of clinical manifestations resulting therefrom have been adequately described.

Part II

THE CHEMICAL ENVIRONMENT,
IN GENERAL

IN CONTRAST to these naturally occurring physical and biological exposures capable of inducing specific susceptibility and manifesting as chronic illness, the man-made chemical environment is a *relatively new* exposure, both racially and individually. Furthermore, whereas the physical and biological environmental excitants are relatively inert as far as humans are concerned, this is far less true of the chemical excitants to be described. Therefore, and in view of the ever-increasing role of *synthetic chemicals* in our lives, it is not surprising that susceptibility to and maladaptation to this comparatively new and relatively unstable chemical environment is a common major cause of advanced clinical syndromes.

There seem to be several reasons why chemical additives, contaminants and drugs have not been recognized as common causes of chronic ills:

1) Since a prolonged period of exposure usually precedes the onset of clinical susceptibility and maladaptation to an environmental excitant and since many pathogenic chemicals are relatively new, perhaps sufficient time has not elapsed for the development or the observation of this phenomenon.

2) Another drawback has been the debate as to whether the involved chemicals are *allergens, irritants* or *toxins;* a difference of opinion that apparently has detracted from the more fundamental facts that specific susceptibility and adaptation are the common denominators of the process. Despite the essential irritant and even toxic nature of some of the agents to be listed, it should be emphasized that the dosages under consideration

[*10*]

are not ordinarily regarded as either irritant or toxic.

3) However, the greatest single deterrent to recognizing the causative role of the chemical environment in chronic illness has been the fact that the most effective diagnostic modus operandi has not been described.

Incidence

Susceptibility to chemical additives and contaminants of air, food, water and biological drugs and chemically derived drugs has been demonstrated to be the leading factor in the causation of chronic illness in approximately *one-third* of the writer's chronically ill patients. It appears to be a contributing factor which cannot be ignored for best results in the management of *another third*. Other statements concerning the relative incidence of this so-called chemical susceptibility problem cannot be made at this time.

Scope

Since this presentation is principally concerned with the factor of *individual susceptibility to the everyday chemical environment,* no attempt will be made to evaluate the effects of toxic or irritant chemical exposures. Neither is this article concerned with the occupational aspects of man's chemical environment other than those peculiar to the household, automobiles, gardens, lawns and other exposures generally common to the majority of individuals. Finally, the aim of this report is to emphasize the interrelationships of the chemical problem as a whole rather than to develop particular facets of it. Exceptions will be made for those constituent parts neither adequately recognized nor fully described. For instance, relatively more space will be devoted to the subject of *indoor chemical air pollution* than with drug sensitivity, upon which extensive reports are available.

Awareness of the totality and potential clinical significance of susceptibility to the chemical environment was not apparent until the opportunity of studying several patients who were unusually susceptible to an exceedingly wide range of environmental chemicals. Information gained from such advanced cases since has been applied advantageously to many less advanced instances.

Two of these early illustrative cases will be reported in detail, since it is helpful for the reader to understand the possible scope of this problem before taking up individual facets of it. However, it should be emphasized that the methods currently recommended have changed considerably from those employed in working out these early cases.

Illustrative Case Reports

Mrs. N. B., physician's wife and former cosmetics sales-woman, 41, was first seen in 1947. Since childhood she has been subject to perennial rhinitis, intermittent canker sores, frequent headaches, hives, chronic fatigue, irritability, tenseness and nervousness. Progressively troublesome coughing and bronchial asthma developed later. Pruritus of her eyelids with edema and circumorbital dermatitis followed each attempt to wear nail polish. She was also highly intolerant to perfumes, certain other scented cosmetics and many drugs. Chronic depression had become increasingly troublesome.

Although shown to be sensitive to house dust and to silk, a test or therapeutic injection of either—even if infinitesimally small—was followed within 15 minutes by nasal stuffiness, coughing and headache. Chocolate, pork and certain other minor foods were suspected; still others were incriminated on the basis of individual food ingestion tests (13). But despite avoidance of incriminated materials, she not only remained chronically sick but continued to develop new symptoms and reactions to new materials. Many of her bizarre reports of suspected agents remained unexplained until the development in 1951 of the point of view presented herein.

For instance, each time she came to Chicago she developed acute coughing, asthma and/or headache shortly after entering the extensive petroleum refinery area in Northwestern Indiana, through which she had to pass. She then *remained* sick if quartered on *lower* floors of Loop hotels or if she attempted to go about at street level; but she *improved* within 24 hours if she remained *above the twentieth floor* in the same area. These responses—markedly accentuated on rainy, humid, foggy or "quiet" days—were subsequently traced to the inhalation of refinery odors in driving into Chicago and to the street-level traffic fumes in the downtown area. Indeed, she had been extremely susceptible to automotive exhausts—

especially those from decelerating and diesel engines. If caught behind a diesel truck or bus while driving, she either stopped, passed it, or even violated whatever traffic regulations were necessary to escape from it.

In addition to immediate coughing, asthma and headache from such exposures, she had been known to develop a state of altered consciousness simulating drunkenness, and a few times had lapsed into an unconscious stupor. Upon three occasions she had slumped at the wheel while driving in such traffic, an accident having been averted only by another person rescuing the steering wheel. Although she experienced less reaction when riding in the front seat, there were only a few automobiles in which she was able to remain unaffected. Another time, while a front seat passenger in a car having a defective muffler, she became progressively sick, then stuporous, whereas other passengers neither reported smelling such fumes nor reacted adversely to them.

More recently, this patient's rhinitis and asthma had increased each year, beginning July 4 and extending throughout the summer. This history, not conforming to local hay fever seasons, finally was traced to the *pine paneling* in her summer home to which she migrated at the *same time* each year. She was also susceptible to the odors of burning pine and various pine-scented materials. She was extremely susceptible to the odors of indoor Christmas trees; evaporating paint containing either turpentine or mineral spirits; lacquer, shellac, varnish and synthetic alcohol.

Upon one occasion she suddenly began to cough and wheeze within a few minutes after entering a hunting lodge which had been heated in advance by means of a fuel-oil stove. This episode remained unexplained until similar heating devices were incriminated under like circumstances. Having previously suspected the odors of her gas kitchen stove and other gas burning home utilities, sponge rubber padding and upholstery and certain flexible plastics, these materials had been discarded prior to her initial visit. After the load of her constant chemical exposures had been reduced, she subsequently reported that she reacted to the presence of gas ranges when visiting other homes; also from sitting on sponge rubber or plastic upholstered furniture; from sleeping on sponge rubber mattresses or pillows, or beds in which mattresses and pillows were covered with plastic encasings.

This patient also developed severe respiratory symptoms and headache when filling plastic bags with food for deep freezing, and when she subsequently ate food frozen in plastic, but not from the same food *before* it had been so stored. Similar reactions were observed from eating food which had been stored in plastic refrigerator dishes or which had been stored in open glass dishes in plastic-lined refrigerators, whereas the same *fresh* food or that stored tightly in *glass* was taken without reaction. From this type of experience, she learned of the superiority of enamel-lined electric refrigerators.

As this patient was known to be sensitive to house dust, one might inquire how dust avoidance was handled in view of reactions to the odors of sponge rubber and plastics. One chair which had been treated with Dust Seal (hydrolyzed mineral oil) had to be removed from her home, as she developed respiratory symptoms each time she sat on it. Reactions to injections of *house dust extract* were subsequently traced to *phenol* employed as a preservative. Her problem of house dust allergy has been handled adequately by general cleanliness, including the frequent cleaning of feather pillows, and injection therapy with phenol-free house dust extracts.

Severe symptoms of the type described, following exposure to perfumes, forced her to give up her work selling cosmetics. Similar symptoms, plus generalized edema and rapid gain in weight, have followed each attempt to wear nylon uniforms, as has contact with certain other synthetic textiles or plastics. Upon three occasions she lapsed into an unconscious stupor immediately after drinking green creme d'menthe. Less severe but similar reactions have also followed ingestion of artificially colored foods: maraschino cherries, mint sauce, frankfurters, bologna, gravies, colored pie and cake frostings and fillings, colored gelatin salads and desserts, ice creams, sherbets, ices, candies, and certain other artificially colored foods and drinks.

Following recognition of the common chemical contaminant factor in these exposures, she inquired why she was able to eat tomatoes from her own garden, whereas commercially canned tomatoes invariably made her sick. Inquiry revealed that she became ill after eating foods canned in *lined tins,* whereas the same *fresh* food or food packed in *unlined tins* or glass did not cause such reaction. Ingestion of commercially available food containing appreciable quantities of *insecticide spray residues* were followed by similar symptoms, whereas the same home grown unsprayed foods were taken with impunity.

— Originally, she was thought to have been sensitive to beef, on the basis of a positive individual food ingestion test with commercially available beef and similar reactions each time beef was eaten. Later, she found that she *could* eat beef raised on a neighbor's farm—beef which had *not* been fed commercially processed feeds; beef which had not been sprayed for fly control or injected with antibiotics, and which had been raised on a farm fertilized only with manure. She has since used *this type* of meat without any trouble. Each attempt to reintroduce foods commercially canned in lined tins, foods known to have been sprayed with insecticides, or beef obtained through commercial channels has preduced *acute* respiratory symptoms, headache or depression.

A similar reaction was induced by the experimental ingestion of the calculated amount of *coal tar dye* (Amaranth No. 2) which would be found in a large serving of gelatin dessert. She also became sick immediately upon inhaling sulfur odors or drinking heavily sulfured or chlorinated water; eating refined cane or beet sugar, or taking aspirin, saccharine, sulfonamides, barbiturates, methadon, meperidine and many other synthetically derived drugs.

Treatment of this patient has consisted of avoiding incriminated exposures as detected. Upon one occasion an acute stuporous depression in which she had been unconscious for several hours was treated effectively by the administration of sodium bicarbonate, intravenously. (The use of this will be described subsequently.) Although she had profited by avoiding as many incriminated chemical exposures as possible, the range of materials involved has made complete avoidance exceedingly difficult. In addition, there are certain regular exposures believed to be perpetuating chronic symptoms that have not been avoided. For instance, she is currently addicted to frequent doses of a synthetic drug employed for *pain relief;* also, she is believed to be reacting to the inhalation of fumes arising from the warm air furnace in her home. At least two similarly affected patients—including the following reported case—reacted acutely to the air in this home when visiting there for only one hour during the winter season.

K. S., a housewife, 44, was first seen in 1953. As a child she usually had a ruddy complexion, was hyperactive and usually ran aimlessly, becoming progressively jittery, irritable and clumsy, with intermittent periods of rhinitis, sick headaches and car sickness. These symptoms usually were treated with aspirin, bromo-seltzer and, later, by antihistaminic drugs. Both chronic and acute effects were accentuated when in the kitchen where she frequently broke dishes and cried when reproached. She much preferred to remain outdoors where, she said, there was "more air." During her entire childhood she was never able to concentrate or study in her home. Her school work was erratic, there being some good days but many others in which she was unable to remain attentive or to recall what she had previously studied. In retrospect, it appears that the clinical picture was related to homes heated with *unvented kerosene stoves,* illuminated by *kerosene lamps,* and in which cooking was invariably done on *kerosene ranges.*

All symptoms became accentuated upon moving to Chicago at the age of 15, and again were heightened immediately after moving into a freshly painted apartment in the fall of 1944. Intermittent colds and bouts of influenza occurred throughout that winter. *Food sensitivity* was suspected for the first time, as evidenced by acute illness after each attempt to eat cherries, although she has since eaten *chemically uncontaminated* cherries with impunity. The following summer in camp, even though eating *all* foods she remained entirely symptom free until the prophylactic administration of sulfonamides, following exposure to scarlet fever. Extreme nausea and listlessness developed immediately.

With the recurrence of rhinitis, bronchitis and influenza-like symptoms coincident with the onset of cool weather in the fall, she was given sulfonamides a second time. This was followed immediately by the onset of an acute generalized rash necessitating discontinuance of this drug. Severe bronchitis progressed to asthma that fall while enrolled in a pottery class. The severity of these respiratory symptoms and the fact that they were accentuated each time she entered the vicinity of the gas-fired pottery kiln necessitated dropping this activity. Throughout that winter she continued with intermittent asthma, unexplained fevers and extreme fatigue for which she received several courses of antibiotics with little, if any, relief.

During the winter of 1945-46 she was said to have had influenza seven times. Because of almost constant headaches, anorexia, nausea and vomiting she lost 25 pounds in one month. During this time she was receiving daily doses of analgesics and barbiturates—a program followed for the next seven years. Coincident with perennial medications she persisted in having *perennial* rather than *seasonal* symptoms. Although she was suspected of having been sensitive to various drugs, there was little change when these were discontinued, singly. All drug therapy was not stopped simultaneously until 1953. In addition to being sensitive to sulfonamides, by this time she had also become aware of violent reactions to procaine, vitamin B and certain antibiotics.

Coincident with moving into an old house and painting its interior in the fall of 1947 there was a marked accentuation of her bronchitis and asthma which continued throughout that winter. A major gas leak about the gas kitchen stove was detected toward spring. Finding that she was able to improve her respiratory symptoms temporarily by inhaling the heated air from the gas oven, she repeated this exposure as often as necessary to control her asthma. Although this regimen afforded *immediate temporary* relief of wheezing, it was associated with an increasing level of headaches, staggering gait, depression and intermittent loss of consciousness. Aching and stiffness of various muscles and joints became so troublesome that she had to be helped from chairs. Most of the three following years she was confined to her bed. During the summer months she improved sufficiently to be outdoors where she seemed to be more comfortable. She also noticed that she was more sick *at her own home* than when visiting in the home of a nearby friend (who happened to have an electric stove in her kitchen). Although this patient had always hated the smell of gas, she had not associated this *daily exposure* with her chronic incapacitating symptoms.

After the usual invalidism through the winter of 1949-50, she was taken to a ranch in the Arizona mountains in April 1950. Within a week she became symptom-free, except for an occasional recurrence of hyperactivity and redness of face followed by headache, severe asthma and residual myalgia and arthritis. In retrospect, she recalled that these reactions occurred only on colder days when the unvented gas wall heater had been turned on.

Upon returning to her former Illinois home where she continued to use gas utilities for four months that summer she immediately became sick and remained so. That fall she returned to Arizona but moved into an apartment heated by open gas burning wall units and equipped with a gas kitchen range. Although she remained fairly well when outdoors, indoors she awakened about three o'clock each morning with nausea, vomiting, headache, swollen throat, dizziness, ataxia and severe depression. This persisted until she could again get outdoors into fresh air.

A year later she moved into a ranch type home having warm air gas central heating, a gas kitchen range and water heater. In looking back, she claims that she remained sick most of the time but invariably improved outdoors. This was attributed by those around her to the beneficial effect of sunshine, since she remained miserable when the sun *didn't* shine (and when indoors with her gas utilities).

As her illness progressed, acute episodes became characterized by aphonia, extreme hyperactivity, ataxia, and confusion suggesting alcoholic intoxication. When hospitalized in such a semi-conscious depressed stupor she improved within a few hours and was relatively symptom-free by the third or fourth day; however, she developed a prompt recurrence of symptoms a few hours after returning home. Upon readmission to the hospital she was often accused of having taken dope or having inflicted her acute attacks upon herself in order to return to the hospital. Several such acute episodes were treated by intravenous procaine; this not only failed to help but seemed to prolong the stupor. She was then treated at home by means of attendants, remaining chronically semi-stuporous, confused and at times hallucinatory. Hearing that she was to be committed to a mental hospital, her brother, a physician, removed her from the state and placed her under the writer's care.

The probable chemical origin of her symptoms was recognized when first seen, although they had not been suspected by the patient or her family. Upon entering an apartment the first night in Chicago she seemed all right, but, coincident with lighting the gas stove to prepare her dinner, she noticed a strong odor of gas and began to feel generally uncomfortable; her eyes and lips burned; face flushed. She became generally excited, ravenously hungry and complained of a bitter taste in her mouth. Although the stove was turned off immediately and windows were opened, there rapidly developed an increasing hoarseness, aphonia, contracture of the left sternocleidomastoid muscle pulling her head to one side, crossing of eyes, ataxia, mental confusion and a sense of floating in space.

After a relatively brief span of rapidly increasing hyperactivity and incoordination she slumped into a semi-conscious stupor during which there were brief intermittent wave-like periods in which she could be aroused or could make her wants known but could not speak. She was alternately chilly and excessively warm. Her respiratory rate remained at 20 and her pulse at 73. As the stupor deepened, she developed intermittent fibrillatory muscle twitchings which rapidly progressed to involve larger muscle groups. This manifested as severe muscle cramps in the calves and later throughout the limbs. Continued marked redness of face, extreme air hunger, upward rolling of eyes, progressive opisthotonus and flailing of extremities requiring constant attendance to avoid self-injury completed the acute picture.

In the absence of additional exposures, the above symptoms leveled off and gradually subsided. Consciousness returned six hours after the onset of this attack, following exposure to a *gas stove* the first time in a week. Her first demand was for water which she drank copiously, but she could not hold the glass. Neither was she able to stand at first; later she was able to walk with assistance, dragging her left foot in a typical ataxic gait. For several hours her left hand was only partially usable. Residual myalgic and arthritic pains persisted for two days; extreme fatigue for another day.

During the following year this patient was observed in many similar attacks, one having been photographed. A neurological consultation at the inception of the stupor phase is quoted: "Deep reflexes are equal and three plus; eyes are rolled upward and crossed; she appears to be semi-stuporous but at times responds to spoken voice, at other times not. No response to painful stimuli. Impression: Cataleptic attack. I would strongly suspect hysteria."

Precipitating causes of similar attacks include the following chemical exposures:

1) *Indoor Chemical Air Contaminants.* Exposure to utility gas

or the combustion products of gas, oil or coal—the most troublesome being exhausts from fuel-oil or gas ranges or room heaters,
gas regrigerators, gas water heaters and gas driers; coal smoke;
warm air heating system odors, irrespective of fuel employed;
odors of oil-impregnated filters of air conditioning equipment and
evaporating oil from certain other equipment such as motors in
electric fans and electric heaters; odors of fresh paint, turpentine,
mineral spirits, synthetic alcohol, detergents, household deodorants, disinfectants, Chlorox, ammonia, adhesive cements, sponge
rubber bedding and padding; certain odorous plastics, including
upholstery; insecticide sprays, napthalein, dichlorobenzene and
certain other insect repellants.

2) *Outdoor Chemical Air Contaminants.* Traffic exhausts,
industrial air pollution—especially odors arising from refineries
and storage tanks; paint manufacture and sulfur processing; insecticide spraying; odors of tarring roofs and roads.

3) *Chemical Additives and Contaminants of Food and Water.*
Foods containing insecticide spray residues, fumigant residues,
certain chemical preservatives, sulfur residues, colored chemical
flavoring or sweetening agents; foods stored in plastic containers
or canned in lined tins; the fats of commercially available beef,
lamb, some chicken and other fowl. Drinking chlorinated water
or eating food which has been standing in it or cooked in it also
causes reactions when otherwise symptom-free.

4) *Synthetic Drugs, Cosmetics and Miscellaneous Chemical
Contacts.* Acute reactions followed the ingestion of acetylsalicylic
acid, sulfonamides, synthetic vitamins; injections of procaine
as well as epinephrine, allergenic extracts or other biological
materials containing phenol or other chemical preservatives. All
cosmetics were suspected except those of biological origin and
free of active synthetic ingredients, scents, colors and bases. Reactions have been traced to wearing Nylon, Dacron and certain
other synthetic textiles; the use of bed linens washed with detergents, dried in gas driers or impregnated with plasti-starch
also have been incriminated.

Manifestations

Since this manuscript is primarily concerned with the description of *chemical environment* and secondarily with the resulting *clinical manifestations,* the latter will be described briefly.

As susceptibility to frequently encountered chemical exposures builds up, the process tends to spread to *related* materials to which exposures also exist. Adaptation to the total load gradually decreases, coincident with the onset of chronic symptoms.

Chronic illness resulting from maladaptation to various parts of the chemical environment may manifest only as eye irritation, rhinitis, burning of the lips and skin, pruritus, bronchitis, mild gastrointestinal or other relatively minor symptoms, localized principally to major points of contact. For instance, if *smog* is the major exposure, eye irritation, running nose and coughing may be the principal symptoms, but if spray residues in foods are primarily involved, manifestations may be largely referable to the gastrointestinal tract.

Later, more severe chronic respiratory symptoms may occur, including nasal obstruction, sinus involvement, severe coughing and bronchial asthma; various dermatoses; a wide range of more troublesome gastrointestinal manifestations, and sometimes urgency and frequency of urination. Mild constitutional symptoms, such as physical and mental fatigue usually accompany the above chronic localized effects. These most frequently manifest as tiredness; a cut-back in former energy; lack of initiative and zest for work; forgetfulness; difficulty in thinking, concentrating and reading comprehension, and sometimes a relative impairment in the sense of humor. Other symptoms which often occur are headaches; various musculoskeletal aching and painful syndromes, including myalgia, fibrositis, bursitis, arthralgia and arthritis; neuritis and certain other neurological manifestations; and such other general effects as edema, palpitation, excessive perspiration, pallor and weakness.

Localized manifestations tend to taper off in the presence of more advanced chronic constitutional syndromes. For instance, there is the chronic level of the so-called "neuroses" characterized by more advanced mental confusion and mild depression. Although manifestations vary considerably, these include a tendency for fixed ideas, one-track thoughts and asocial attitudes; morose, sullen, seclusive, and sometimes hostile and paranoid behavior;

negativeness to suggestion; and "dopiness," grogginess and an indifference to one's surroundings, sometimes approaching lethargy.

Combinations and accentuations of the above symptoms merge with the level of the so-called "psychoses" which are characterized by severe depression, disorientation, regression, and sometimes by hallucinations, delusions and amnesia. The characteristic alternating tendency of these four levels of chronic "hangover-like" effects, first noted by Savage (14), has been the subject of a recent report by the writer (15).

However, if a person is separated from causative environmental exposures perpetuating such chronic "hangover" effects, he tends to improve by retracing these levels of reaction. Although his "hangovers" are first accentuated, he tends to become relatively symptom-free within a few days—the time required depending on the *depth of reaction* and *completeness of the avoidance program*. This changes a partially adapted stage (usually somewhere between stages II and III) to a non-adapted stage (I).

Reexposure to a previously avoided causative excitant to which susceptibility exists now tends to induce an immediate acute reaction which is employed for *diagnostic* purposes, as will be described. The initial "pick up" phase is characterized by *four depths* of *reaction,* which are predominately motor in type, and a delayed "hangover" phase similar to those previously described, briefly. A given reaction may proceed to any one of these depths before merging with and then being superseded by approximately the same "hangover" level.

Initially, one may become active, alert and relatively stimulated but otherwise remain symptom-free. This is the stage of response which the *specifically adapted* person often maintains for many months or years as a result of oft-repeated exposures. His lesser grade "hangovers" only manifest at this stage if such a frequently repeated exposure happens to be avoided, but, in such an event, *reexposure* quickly picks him up again—a status which he comes to regard as "normalcy."

After a time, susceptibility increases, adaptation decreases, and "pick ups" come to be characterized by energetic bursts of physical activity and hyperactivity in which a patient remains nervous, keyed-up and irritable for several hours. Nearby persons often are involved in inter-personal difficulties that are dubbed "emotional upsets." These, in turn, frequently are interpreted erroneously as "causes" of subsequently developing "hangover" effects.

More intense reactions may occur in which a person is flushed in the face, clumsy, ataxic, argumentative and aggressive. Here there is an even greater tendency to involve other individuals, but the victim's behavior—so obviously abnormal at this point—is not as apt to be taken seriously by others as in lesser but similar reactions.

Or, there may develop a state of uncontrollable agitation and excitement. This is characterized by rhythmical muscle contractures ranging from muscle twitching to flailing of extremities and epileptiform seizures. Transitory blackouts or more prolonged loss of consciousness may occur. Early "pick up" stages are apt to be compressed into auras or telescoped completely in the initial phase of such rapidly advancing severe reactions. Alternating waves of excessive thirst, voracious appetite and air hunger often typify these "pick up" phases of acute reactions. This may manifest as eating or drinking binges (16) in earlier phases of reaction, or, in the more advanced stages, by extreme air hunger—a frantic desire for more air or to get outdoors. This may become so intense that a patient will fight any person who interferes with the fulfillment of such overpowering desire.

If a person living at any given "hangover" level is exposed to a substance to which he is susceptible and at least partially adapted, and if the dose is several times *larger* than that to which he is accustomed, he is apt to manifest an acute immediate reaction, becoming relatively stimulated, hyperactive, drunk-like or uncontrollably excited. In general, such a "pick up" occurs at approximately the same depth of reaction as the "hangover" level to which he is ordinarily accustomed, although it may descend a depth lower before returning to its former level. This type of alternation between acute "pick ups" and chronic "hangovers" is epitomized in the most extreme cases by behavior descriptively similar to manic and depressed phases of the manic-depressive psychosis. Reactions at lesser levels may be simply pictured as *less advanced* responses of similar type. These patterns of reaction, previously described only preliminarily, are being reported in extenso (17,18).

Diagnosis

Susceptibility to the chemical environment is a difficult diagnosis to establish because of the wide individual variations in its manifestations and its potential scope. This is reasonable since no two persons have the same exposures or ability to adapt to them. Indeed, there are valid objections as to whether susceptibility to the chemical environment should be regarded as a clinical entity. But the common genesis of the excitants, the general pattern of the response as described, and the tendency for susceptibility to involve an increasing number of facets to which chronic exposures exists make it desirable to consider the subject in its *totality*.

This common genesis includes the original sources of the hydrocarbons—coal, oil and gas. If it is permissible to carry the process back another step, and if one accepts the geological concept that conifir forests were the precursors of these materials, such an interpretation is in keeping with the close association of the clinical effects of *pine and its combustion products* with those of coal, oil and gas and their combustion products and derivatives.

History

Although individuals may be aware of susceptibility to one or more of the facets of the constellation of exposures to be described, a chronically ill person rarely ever knows the total number of chemical excitants impinging on his health. Consequently, the history is of only limited value except in the most advanced cases. Due to its scope, the history is best recorded by means of a questionnaire; this comprehensive one, used by the writer, has not been previously published, except for the incorporation of an early form of it into the questionnaire employed by Brown and Colombo (19).

It is suggested that the new patient fill out the questionnaire *before* he becomes acquainted with the scope and possible significance of this problem.

QUESTIONNAIRE

CHEMICAL ADDITIVES and CONTAMINANTS of AIR, FOOD, WATER, DRUGS & COSMETICS

By Theron G. Randolph, M. D.   720 N. Michigan Ave., Chicago 11, Ill.

Date _____ Name _____   Home Address _____

CIRCLE or FILL IN the following: Sex _____ Age _____

Education		Marital Status	Occupation
Highest school year:		Single	Work Region Work Address
1 2 3 4 5 6 7 8	1 2 3 4	Married	City Distance from work
Elementary	High	Widowed	Suburban Travel by:
1 2 3 4	1 2 3 4	Separated	Small town Car Train Other
College	Graduate	Divorced	Rural Bus Walking

Home

Type	If multiple dwelling	Region	Garage
Single House	What floor? ____	City residential	In separate unattached
Double House	How long have you	City industrial	building
Apartment	lived there? ____	Suburban	With inside passageway
Hotel		Small town	between house & garage
Trailer		Rural	In basement of house

Heating & Ventilation of Home

Type	Fuel	Furnace Location	Air Conditioning	Kitchen Exhaust
Electric, heat pump	Electric	Basement	Window units	Fan
Electric, radiant	Gas	Main floor	Central system	Yes
Hot water or steam	Oil	Utility room	Filters - oiled,	No
Warm Air	Coal	Open	Unoiled,	Kitchen Door
Space heaters	Wood	Closed	Electrostatic	Usually left open
Fireplaces	Other ____		Activated carbon	Usually closed

Utilities

Range	Refrigerator		Deep Freeze	Clothes Dryer	Water Heater
Electric	Type	Food Storage	Electric	Electric	Electric
Gas	Electric	In Glass	Gas	Gas	Gas
Oil	Gas	In enamel ware	Age ____	Age ____	Part of furnace
Age ____	Age ____	In plastic			Age ____

Furnishings and Household Maintenance

Upholstery Coverings	Padding	Mattresses	Pillows	Rugs	Rug Pads
Cotton Silk	Cotton	Cotton	Feather	Wool	Plastic
Linen Wool	Hair	Rubber	Rubber	Cotton	Rubber
Synthetic fabrics	Rubber	Plastic covered	Kapok	Synthetic	Hair
Plastic	Other ____	Other ____	Dacron	Natural fiber	
			Plastic covered	Rubber or	
				Plastic backed	

Curtains	Cleansers	Deodorants & Disinfectants	Laundry		Furniture
Cotton silk	Soap	Air wick	Soap	Plastic starch	Polish
Wool linen	Detergents	Lysol	Bleaches	Cornstarch	Yes No
Plastic	Scouring pwd.	Pine-Sol	Ammonia	Dryer	Floor Wax
Synthetic mat.	with bleach	Others ____	Detergents	Electric	Yes No
	Ammonia			Gas	

(Continued)

--2--

CHEMICAL ADDITIVES AND CONTAMINANTS -- Continued

Miscellaneous

Insect Control	Drinking Water	Sense of Smell	Ability to Detect Leaking Gas	When Wind is Blowing from Industrial Areas Are your Symptoms
Sprays	Spring or well	Very acute		
Moth Balls	Softened	Normal	Acute	
Moth Crystals	Chlorinated	Poor	Normal or average	Increased
Exterminators	Fluoridated	Absent	Poor or absent	Unchanged

* * * * * *

WHAT IS YOUR REACTION TO THE FOLLOWING?   CHECK ONE:

LIKE NEU- DIS- MADE
TRAL LIKE SICK
FROM

COAL, OIL, GAS & COMBUSTION PRODUCTS:

1. Massive outdoor exposures to coal smoke ....
2. Smoke in steam railroad stations, train sheds and yards ..
3. Smoke from coal burning stoves, furnaces or fireplaces ..
4. Odors of natural gas fields ....
5. Odors of escaping utility gas ....
6. Odors of burning utility gas ....
7. Odors of gasoline ....
8. Garage fumes and odors ....
9. Automotive or motor boat exhausts ....
10. Odor of naphtha, cleaning fluids or lighter fluids ....
11. Odor of recently cleaned clothing, upholstery or rugs ....
12. Odor of naphtha-containing soaps ....
13. Odor of nail polish or nail polish remover ....
14. Odor of brass, metal or shoe polishes ....
15. Odor of fresh newspapers ....
16. Odor of kerosene ....
17. Odor of kerosene or fuel-oil burning lamps or stoves .....
18. Odor of kerosene or fuel-oil burning space heaters or
       furnaces ....
19. Diesel engine fumes from trains, buses, trucks or boats ..
20. Lubricating greases or crude oil ....
21. Fumes from automobiles burning an excessive amount of oil
22. Fumes from burning greasy rags ....
23. Odors of smudge pots as road markers or frost inhibitors

MINERAL OIL, VASELINE, WAXES, AND COMBUSTION PRODUCTS

1. Mineral oil as contained in hand lotions and medications
2. Mineral oil as a laxative ....
3. Cold cream or face or foundation cream ....
4. Vaseline, petroleum jelly or petrolatum-containing ointments
5. Odors of floor, furniture or bowling alley wax ....
6. Odors of glass wax or similar glass cleaners ....
7. Fumes from burning wax candles ....
8. Odors from dry garbage incinerators ....

(Continued)

-- 3 --

	LIKE	NEU-TRAL	DIS-LIKE	MADE SICK FROM

WHAT IS YOUR REACTION TO THE FOLLOWING?   CHECK ONE:

ASPHALTS, TARS, RESINS & DYES

1. Fumes from tarring roofs and roads ....
2. Asphalt pavements in hot weather ....
3. Tar-containing soaps, shampoos and ointments ....
4. Odors of inks, carbon paper, typewriter ribbons & stencils
5. Dyes in clothing and shoes ....
6. Dyes in cosmetics (lipstick, mascara, rouge, powder, other)

DISINFECTANTS, DEODORANTS & DETERGENTS

1. Odor of public or household disinfectants and deodorants
2. Odor of phenol (carbolic acid) or Lysol ....
3. Phenol-containing lotions or ointments ....
4. Injectable materials containing phenol as a preservative
5. Fumes from burning creosote-treated wood (railroad ties)..
6. Household detergents ....

RUBBER

1. Odor of rubber or contact with rubber--gloves, elastic in
   clothing, girdles, brassieres, garters, etc.............
2. Odor of sponge rubber bedding, rug pads, typewriter pads .
3. Odor of rubber based paint ....
4. Odor of rubber tires, automotive accessories stores, etc..
5. Odor of rubber-backed rugs and carpets ....
6. Fumes of burning rubber ....

PLASTICS, SYNTHETIC TEXTILES, FINISHES & ADHESIVES

1. Odor of or contact with plastic upholstery, table cloths,
   book covers, pillow covers, shoe bags, hand bags ....
2. Odor of plastic folding doors or interiors of automobiles
3. Odor of or contact with plastic spectacle frames, dentures
4. Odor of plastic products in department or specialty stores
5. Nylon hose and other nylon wearing apparel ....
6. Dacron or Orlon clothing or upholstery ....
7. Rayon or cellulose acetate clothing or upholstery ....
8. Odor of or contact with adhesive tape ....
9. Odor of plastic cements ....

ALCOHOLS, GLYCOLS, ALDEHYDES, ESTERS & DERIVED SUBSTANCES

1. Odor of rubbing alcohol ....
2. Alcohols or glycols as contained in medications ....
3. Odor of varnish, lacquer or shellac ....

(Continued)

-- 4 --

WHAT IS YOUR REACTION TO THE FOLLOWING? CHECK ONE:	LIKE	NEU-TRAL	DIS-LIKE	MADE SICK FROM

ALCOHOLS, CLYCOLS, ALDEHYDES, KETONES, ESTERS & DERIVED SUBSTANCES - Continued

4. Odor of after shaving lotions, hair tonics or hair oils ...
5. Odor of window cleaning fluids ....
6. Odor of paint or varnish thinned with mineral solvents ....
7. Odor of banana oil ....
8. Odor of scented soap and shampoo ....
9. Odor of perfumes and colognes ....
10. Odor of Spray Net and other hair dressings ....
11. Fumes from burning incense ....

MISCELLANEOUS

1. Air conditioning ....
2. Ammonia fumes ....
3. Odor of moth balls ....
4. Odor of insect repellant candles ....
5. Odor of termite extermination treatment ....
6. Odor of DDT containing insecticide sprays ....
7. Odor of Chlordane, Lindane, Parathione, Dieldrin and
    other insecticide sprays ....
8. Odor of the fruit and vegetable sections of supermarkets ..
9. Odor of chlorinated water ....
10. Drinking of chlorinated water ....
11. Fumes of chlorine gas ....
12. Odor of Chlorox and other hypochlorite bleaches ....
13. Fumes from sulfur processing plants ....
14. Fumes of sulfur dioxide ....

PINE

1. Odor of Christmas trees & other indoor evergreen
    decorations ....
2. Odor of knotty pine interiors ....
3. Odor from sanding or working with pine or cedar woods .....
4. Odor of cedar scented furnish polish ....
5. Odor of pine scented household deodorants ....
6. Odor of pine scented bath oils, shampoos, or soaps ....
7. Odor of turpentine or turpentine-containing paints ....
8. Fumes from burning pine cones or wood ....

(Continued)

— 5 —

CIRCLE CLASSES OF DRUGS, or DRUGS, IF SUSPECTED.   NAME OTHERS NOT LISTED.

Analgesics	Adrenalin (epinephrine)	_____
Androgens	Aminophyllin	_____
Anesthetics, local	Aspirin (Bufferin, Empirin)	_____
Anesthetics, general	Barbiturates	_____
Antibiotics	Codeine	_____
Anticoagulants	Demerol	_____
Anticonvulsants	Ephedrine	_____
Antihistaminics	Ether	_____
Antispasmodics	Iodides	_____
Asthma remedies	Mineral Oil	_____
Diuretics	Morphine	_____
Estrogens	Novocaine	_____
Headache remedies	Penicillin	_____
Laxatives	Phenobarbital	_____
Opiates	Phenolphthalein	_____
Sedatives	Saccharine	_____
Steroids	Stilbestriol	_____
Tranquilizers	Sucaryl	_____
Vaccines	Sulfonamides	_____
Vitamins	Vaseline	_____

DRUGS CURRENTLY BEING USED - CIRCLE IF SUSPECTED

_____   _____   _____
_____   _____   _____
_____   _____   _____

Currently used Dentifrice   Currently used Mouthwash   Others

_____   _____   _____

Currently used Cosmetics (Name brands, if possible).   Circle if suspected

Deodorant _____	For Women	For Men
Toilet soap _____	Face Powder _____	Electric pre-shave
Shampoo _____	Dusting Powder _____	
Hand Lotion _____	Lipstick _____	After shaving lotion
Cold cream _____	Foundation cream _____	
Contraceptive _____	Nail polish _____	Hair Oil _____
_____	Perfume _____	
_____	Cologne _____	Others _____
_____	Mascara _____	
_____	Eyebrow pencil _____	_____
	Cold Wave _____	
	Permanent _____	_____
	Hair tint _____	
	Douche _____	

(Continued)

<u>CIRCLE</u> THE FOODS SUSPECTED

1. a) Apple, cherry, peach, apricot, nectarine, pear, plum, olive, current, persimmon, strawberry, cranberry, raspberry, blueberry, boysenberry, pineapple, rhubarb, grape, orange, grapefruit, lemon, tangerine.

   b) Brussels sprouts, broccoli, cauliflower, cabbage, head lettuce, tomato, celery, asparagus, spinach, beet greens, chard, mustard greens, endive, escarole, leaf lettuce, romaine, Chinese cabbage, artichoke.

   c) Lamb, beef, pork, chicken, turkey, duck.

2. Dates, figs, shelled nuts, raisins, prunes, other dried fruit; wheat, corn, rye, barley, rice, oats, dried peas, dried beans, lentils.

3. White flour.

4. Peach, apricot, nectarine; fresh apple, fresh apricot, fresh peach, French fried potatoes; molasses, dried fruit, melon, citrus candied peel, fruit marmalade; dried apple, dried pear, dried peach, dried apricot, raisin, prune, corn syrup, corn sugar, cornstarch, corn oil.

5. Creme d' menthe, maraschino cherries, Jello, mint sauce, ice cream, sherbet, hard candy; frostings and fillings of pies and cakes; wieners, bologna, cheese, butter, oleomargarine, orange, sweet potato, Irish potato, root beer, pop, cola drinks.

6. Saccharine, Sucaryl (sodium cyclomate).

7. Banana, orange; apple, pear; coffee; cane sugar, beet sugar.

8. Carrot, parsnip, turnip, tomato, mixed shredded greens; citrus fruit.

9. Rutabaga, parsnip, turnip, green pepper, apple, orange, grapefruit, tangerine, lemon, cucumber, eggplant.

10. Triscuits, cocoanut.

11. Turkey, chicken, duck, eggs, beef, lamb, pork, fish.

12. Chlorinated drinking water; fluoridated drinking water; chlorinated and fluoridated drinking water.

* * * * * * * *

Do you smoke ... cigarettes _____   Pipe _____ Cigars _____
Age you started to smoke   _____   Age you last quit smoking _____
Was it difficult to stop?   _____   Number of smokes per day _____

What is your maximum weight? _____ Your present weight? _____

Interpretation of the Questionnaire

Although there is no single question of paramount importance, the one referring to the ability to *detect escaping gas* deserves special emphasis. Provided a patient has at least an average sense of smell and if he admits of an acute ability to detect the odor of escaping utility gas (i.e., as contrasted with others similarly exposed), this suggests *susceptibility* to this aspect of the chemical problem. However, a negative answer to this question, attributable to anosmia, does not rule out susceptibility to indoor chemical air pollution, of which exposure to odors or derivatives of utility gas is the most important constituent. The next most important questions are those dealing with coal smoke, solvent odors, motor exhausts, tar odors, perfumes, scented cosmetics, drugs and the *first* set of questions concerning *foods*.

In general, it may be said that new patients tend to underestimate the significance of the chemical environment as it effects their health. Only those excitants in which the amount per dose or the regularity of dosage are highly variable are apt to be suspected. Moreover, only those persons whose susceptibility is advanced and whose involvement is widespread are apt to indicate that they are "made sick from" these exposures. The majority, *subsequently* found susceptible to major facets of the chemical environment, most commonly indicate merely a "dislike" when answering this questionnaire. Some of those adapted to one or more of the excitants listed may indicate that they "like" the material in question, especially if they are regularly exposed to it. At least certain patients answering in this manner have been observed to react to an isolated or relatively massive dose of the same material. When a person notices no obvious change upon exposure or is indifferent to it, he is inclined to answer "neutral" or to leave the question unanswered.

The major use of the questionnaire is to determine whether the patient should be maneuvered in respect to his surroundings —including the involved part of the diet—in an attempt to demonstrate the existence of susceptibility to aspects of the chemical environment. The more such a questionnaire is used, the greater the latitude in interpreting the significance of how it is answered.

For instance, answers and comments that at first glance appear to the doctor to be inconsequential are often highly significant when compared with later demonstrations of causation.

Comprehensive Environmental Control

Since a history—including an answered questionnaire—cannot be entirely relied upon, and since there are *few* physical and practically *no* laboratory findings that are useful, the diagnosis of the existence of susceptibility to the chemical environment depends principally on observations of a patient as he is *maneuvered* in respect to his *environment*. Since this chemical problem most frequently *coexists* with susceptibility to foods, drugs, dust, pollens and other inhaled particles, the most accurate method of demonstrating the causes of chronic illness is to *observe* the patient while multiple suspected and probable environmental exposures are being avoided, then subsequently returned, one at a time. This technique—soundly based on the principle of changing adapted to non-adapted responses—culminated in the following program of *comprehensive environmental control* and subsequent test reexposures (3,4).

Patients are fasted in hospital quarters relatively free of chemical odors and fumes as well as pollens, spores, danders and dusts. An isolated portion of the hospital devoted to this work is preferred. Indoor air pollution is controlled as far as possible by means of passing incoming air through activated carbon and mechanical and/or electrostatic filters. Patients avoid all drugs, cosmetics, tobacco and synthetic wearing apparel and drink only spring water.

Symptoms tend to be accentuated at first, usually reaching a peak on the third or fourth day. Chronic manifestations resulting from foods previously eaten regularly then tend to improve; those from susceptibility to chemical additives and contaminants of foods and those from maintenance doses of synthetic drugs improve more slowly. Chronic reactions from foods per se (that is, chemically less contaminated sources) usually start to improve by the fourth day (16). As might be expected by their previous description, greater depths of chronic "hangovers" subside more slowly than less advanced reactions. Although the average duration of the fast is between five and six days, it is sometimes necessary to continue it for ten days and occasionally longer.

Indications for breaking the fast are a relative absence of or a marked decrease in previous chronic symptoms for a period of at least 24 hours; satisfactory sleep, and a stabilization of the pulse rate at a significantly lower level. The fast is usually broken by a meal of unsuspected fish or seafood, chemically uncontaminated insofar as possible. Other foods known not to be significantly contaminated chemically are returned one at a time, preferably not more frequently than twice daily. This routine incorporates the principles of Rinkel's individual food ingestion test (13) and favors the observation of both immediate and delayed objective and subjective effects. Pre- and post-ingestion pulse determinations, as recommended by Coca (21), aid in interpreting borderline reactions.

After all foods used once in three days, or more frequently, have been tested in this way, susceptibility to chemical additives and contaminants in the diet is investigated. This is done by feeding seldom-eaten foods known to contain chemical additives and/or contaminants in *three daily feedings* for at least *two days*. These foods are selected because of their spray residues and chemical contamination arising from can linings, fumigation, fungicides, sulfur treatment and other ways to be described; and because of their availability in chemically *uncontaminated* form as *controls*. They consist of canned blueberries sweetened with Sucaryl, canned peaches, canned dark red cherries, canned salmon, canned tuna, frozen broccoli, frozen cauliflower, frozen spinach, raw apple, raw celery and the outside leaves of head lettuce.

In instances of extreme susceptibility, acute reactions may follow the first ingestion of chemically contaminated foodstuffs, but two days and sometimes longer periods of cumulative ingestion may be necessary before a susceptible person manifests convincing symptoms. At times, the immediate effects of a chemically contaminated diet may be stimulatory. This phase is then followed by the recurrence of any of the localized or constitutional chronic symptom syndromes previously listed.

It is important to emphasize that susceptibility to foods per se or to their chemical additives and contaminants may give rise to *identical* symptoms. Although either may occur alone, they most commonly coexist. However, the over-all effects of the chemical additives and contaminants of the diet are apt to be more toxic, cumulative and associated with greater depths of clinical reaction than ordinarily occurs from susceptibility to foods *per se*.

As soon as the patient and observers are convinced of the presence of acute reactions following test feedings, the gastro-intestinal tract is emptied by means of saline laxatives or enemas; these details will be presented subsequently.

Then with the patient on a compatible intake of food and water and avoiding all drugs, he is returned successively to his home, his former water supply, work and avocations. A recurrence of reactive symptoms during the first 48 hours at home usually indicates susceptibility to *indoor chemical air pollutants*, house dust, animal danders, silk or other home exposures to which susceptibility exists. The most important of these home sources are chemical air pollutants. Details of how these constituent chemical exposures are incriminated will be illustrated by means of case reports after the exposures themselves have been described.

Part III

AIR POLLUTION

WHETHER A person is aware of the impingement of chemical air pollution on his health and behavior depends principally on: 1) his degree of susceptibility and 2) frequency of exposure to such agents. Since this presentation is principally concerned with the highly susceptible, intermittency or constancy of exposure becomes the most important variable in the ability of both patients and physicians to recognize the causative roles of environmental chemicals.

Many other writers (19,20,21,22,23,24,25,26) either described or reported the clinical effects of intermittent air-borne chemical exposures, but the concept that a given person might be susceptible to many materials of *common chemical genesis* was slow to be appreciated. Vaughan (27) was impressed with the relationship between artificialities of the environment and diet of man and allergy. Coca (24) and Brown and Colombo (19) listed odors of utility gas, kerosene, and other solvents including evaporating paint, motor exhausts, wood and coal smoke and newsprint odors as excitants of clinical reactions.

Acute immediate reactions occurring in previously symptom-free out-of-town patients upon entering Chicago usually are readily detected. Indeed, a study of the problem of urban air pollution was prompted by the observation that certain patients living to the east and northeast of Chicago invariably became sick during and after passing through an area containing refineries, steel mills, chemical and paint manfucturing plants. Some noticed only mucous membrane irritation. Others became nervous, jittery, irritable and hyperactive initially with delayed rhinitis, bronchitis, asthma, fatigue, headache or painful musculoskeletal syndromes. A few extreme cases became drunk-like initially before

[*35*]

lapsing into stuporous depressions. Because of the acuity of these reactions in previously unexposed persons, some drove an extra 50 miles in order to avoid this area when entering Chicago. Fortunately, with new roads decreasing exposure time and the use of *activated carbon filters,* the most susceptible may now drive through this region without reaction.

Once the immediate and delayed phases of this clinical picture attributable to intermittent air-borne chemical exposure had been recognized, Chicago residents manifesting similar but more chronic symptoms were studied. Gradually over the past decade the apparent full range of impinging chemical exposures as well as their clinical effects became evident.

It should be emphasized that the geography and weather of this region favor an intermittency of atmospheric pollution and facilitate the investigation of this problem. 1) East winds from Lake Michigan frequently interrupt other winds, thus intermittently clearing the blanket of polluted air overhanging the city. 2) The correlation of clinical symptoms with wind direction is facilitated here by the location of the major industrial installations on one side of the city. 3) The uncommon occurrence of the meterological phenomenon of inversion, the common presence of relatively non-polluted turbulent winds from any quarter and the absence of natural obstructions to winds also favor intermittency of exposure and acute reactions. Although these factors tend to decrease the extent and chronicity of illness, due to susceptibility to chemical exposures, and to aid its detection, Chicago still has a *major outdoor air pollution problem.* But when this knowledge was applied to instances of chronic illness in patients known to be susceptible to diverse chemical exposures, it soon became apparent that outdoor chemical air pollution accounted for *only a portion* of the morbidity of chemically susceptible individuals.

Other readily apparent portions of the chemical environment impinging on susceptible persons consisted of certain *intermittently used* synthetic chemical drugs, cosmetics, and such variable personal contacts as exposure to the odors of fresh paint and solvents, insecticides, perfumes, et cetera. In fact, the total effects of such readily detectible intermittent exposures might be likened to the visible part of an iceberg.

It was not until patients suspected of having the chemical problem were studied by means of *comprehensive environmental control* (3,4) that the writer became aware of the causative roles of related but less often suspected chemical exposures. These might be likened to the *submerged* portion of an iceberg. As a result of this experience, the preponderant significance of *indoor chemical air pollution* became apparent. At least in the Chicago area—and similar conditions apparently exist elsewhere—*indoor* chemical air pollution is a more important cause of chronic debilitating illness than chemical pollution of the *outdoor* atmosphere. Indeed, it is the most subtle to recognize and, singly, the most important phase of the total chemical problem. It must be brought under control before the clinical effects of other facets of the chemical environment may be correctly appraised.

Other hidden portions of the problem comprise such exposures as *chemical additives* and *contaminants* of the *diet, water supplies* and *biological drugs* as well as maintenance dosage of synthetic drugs or daily contact with synthetic textiles and certain other personal contacts. Whereas the clinical effects of indoor chemical air pollution are most troublesome in winter months and are usually confused with the effects of exposure to house dust, it is the "maintenance" doses of chemicals in food, water, drugs, cosmetics and some personal contacts which, in their totality, constitute never-ending and usually unsuspected sources of exposure.

When the clinical effects of these usually hidden facets of the chemical environment were demonstrated in susceptible persons, the proportion of their illness attributable to previously suspected, more readily apparent chemical exposures changed markedly. Such a change is often indicated by having the diagnosed and controlled patient *re-check* his original questionnaire in *red pencil*. In other words, the full range and clinical significance of the pathogenic chemical exposures for a given individual are not appreciated until *after* avoidance of the chemical environment in its totality and reexposure to its constituent parts. Although the chemical problem must be recognized and treated in respect to all of its facets—and each patient presents a highly individualized constellation of susceptibilities to such facets—it is necessary to present the subject in sections.

A.   INDOOR CHEMICAL AIR CONTAMINATION

Since a knowledge of indoor chemical air pollution is a *must* before attempting to interpret the clinical effects of other chemical exposures, the major sources of air pollution in homes and public places will be described and their relative importance discussed.

Should the reader be concerned with the scope of the chemical environment and the negative incriminatory approach in the body of this article, a positive approach in the form which may be used for instruction of patients will be outlined as a summary.

Fuels, Solvents and their Combustion Products

Fuels

Storage of hydrocarbon fuels in the basements of homes is a potential hazard for chemical susceptible patients. Kerosene, used to wet down coal to control dust in delivery, slowly volatilizes and contaminates the air of the basement. There is also a troublesome odor arising from oil storage tanks located in the basement, as well as the additional hazard that they may be overflowed in filling. Once a basement floor has been flooded with fuel-oil, this odor tends to remain for several months or even years, and may necessitate abandonment of such a home. Also, most fuel-oil installations—whether furnaces or space heaters—impart a characteristic odor. Although more odorous when operating, there may be a sufficient odor when not operating to cause symptoms in a highly susceptible person.

Despite the fact utility gas is the cleanest of the readily available fuels, it is also the most hazardous for the majority of chemical susceptible patients. It seems to make little difference whether artificial or natural gas is used, although the relatively high pressures under which natural gas is currently delivered may increase this hazard, especially if home installations have been designed for *lower* pressures. As a consequence, every joint and turn in a utility gas line is a potential and oft-times an actual point of *slight leakage*. Utility gas, being lighter than air, tends to rise from the basement or kitchen through the remainder of the house. The greater the amount of piping and number of outlets, the more pilots and other automatic devices on gas utilities, the greater the potentiality and probability of leakage.

Chronic symptoms may be maintained in the highly susceptible patient living in a gas utility home. This is due to *leakage
of unburned gas,* even though all pilots are turned off, no gas is
burned, and despite the report of the utility company that gas
leaks cannot be detected. Devices for detecting gas leaks are
relatively unsatisfactory and are no match for the extreme susceptibility of certain individuals. *Acute reactions* have been induced
in such persons when returning to such a home after a period of
absence during which the patient in question had not been
exposed to utility gas and related chemical exposures, and when
relatively symptom-free at the time of such a reexposure.

Combustion Products of Fuels

Coal burning stoker furnaces sometimes burn back into the
coil stoking mechanism and contaminate basement air. Coal
burning in open fireplaces is apt to puff at times, discharging
a greater quantity of gas and smoke than may be drawn off by the
chimney. A downdraft through an unused fireplace from a double
chimney containing both fireplace and furnace flues, may carry
combustion products from the furnace or incinerator which may
foul living quarters and cause serious unsuspected reactions. This
may be obviated by keeping a fire in the fireplace when an adjacent flue is being used under atmospheric conditions favoring
such downdrafts.

The fuel-oil-burning space heater and kitchen range are *major
causes* of indoor air pollution and respiratory symptoms, as reported by Brown (20). In the writer's experience (7,18) they are
also common causes of other symptoms, especially depressions
and musculoskeletal painful syndromes. Fortunately, these installations are less common than formerly.

Indoor air pollution arising from the combustion of furnace
fuels seems to depend more on the type and location of the
furnace than the type of *fuel* used. Warm air furnaces are more
troublesome than other types, even though they may be in good
mechanical repair. This statement is based on the *clinical experience* of the change-over from warm air furnaces to hot water
or steam systems in homes of over 50 patients and supervising the

moving of approximately 100 families from warm-air-heated homes to those heated electrically or by means of hot water or steam systems.

Warm air systems may pollute the air of basements by the emission of combustion products through draft apertures as a result of "puffing" each time the gas-fired furnace turns on. Major leaks between the combustion and warm air chambers of the furnace are not uncommon. It is also known that warm air furnaces result in more turbulance and dust disposal than occurs with the use of certain other types of heating equipment. But the speed with which some chemically susceptible persons react to being in the draft of a warm air register as the furnace in good mechanical repair turns on, suggests some additional mechanism. Since these observations have been made with dust-sensitive patients and are more pronounced in cold weather, there is a possibility that an additional toxic factor may be imparted to dust-laden air as it passes over an extremely hot furnace dome. In a few instances, these apparent reactions to "fried dust" have been lessened by the installation of electrostatic filters in the duct system of the furnace. This subject is in urgent need of more detailed investigation.

Air contamination of the home, resulting either from fuels or their combustion products, is relatively increased in basement apartments or in living quarters directly *over* furnace rooms. Indeed, the location of the furnace, irrespective of its type or the fuel used, is of utmost importance. The worst location is in the center of the main floor of a ranch-type home or in an open utility room on the same floor as the living quarters. The ideal location for a furnace—and the only one recommended—is *outside* of the living quarters. This means either in the garage, in a separate room between the house and the garage, or in a completely exteriorized room adjacent to the house which is entered only from the outside. When so located and without direct communication with the house (except for the entrance of the hot water or steam pipes) there seems to be little choice between the use of coal, oil or gas fuels as long as warm water or steam central heating is employed. Although electric heating is preferable, any type of room heating unit containing motor-driven fans is not desirable, as the heat of the unit apparently volatilizes the oil of the fan motor, and this, apparently, induces symptoms in certain highly susceptible persons.

Preliminary evidence suggests that the relatively "cool" heat provided by heat pump electrical installations is preferable to the presence of extraordinarily hot electrical resistance coils. In this connection, two-stage controls of baseboard electrical heating systems are preferable to one-stage controls, since with the former the temperature of the home is maintained most of the time by means of less hot electrical resistance units (28).

Second to such relatively low temperature electrical heating installations, hot water systems are slightly preferable to steam heat, since the volatility of chlorinated-fluoridated water may be responsible for inducing chronic symptoms in certain persons.

Although the installation of mechanical and electrostatic filters in warm air heating systems is helpful in removing dust and other particles, they do *not* remove odors and fumes. In the homes in which this has been tried, installing activated carbon filters in warm air systems in conjunction with the use of electrostatic filters has been less satisfactory than changing to a relatively "cool" type of electric heating or to hot water systems in which the source of combustion is *outside* the living quarters.

The gas-fired kitchen stove's contribution to air contamination of the modern American home is so preponderant that it must first be removed from the premises before other local sources of indoor air pollution can be evaluated. This statement is based on the writer's experience in causing to be permanently removed over 500 such kitchen ranges from the homes of patients susceptible to chemical odors and fumes. One of the most amazing results of this experience is that the writer has *not* received a major complaint from this group of patients regarding the expense of such a move. Once the indications for the move are present and the patient complies with the advice, resulting *clinical improvement* apparently has justified the expenditure.

Air contamination arising from the gas kitchen range *cannot be adequately eliminated* by such part-way measures as increasing ventilation in the kitchen, keeping the kitchen door closed, installing a kitchen exhaust fan, turning off the stove's pilots, disconnecting the stove but leaving it in the room, or even by turning off the gas at the point where the gas line enters the house. Although any or all of these measures may be helpful, their relative ineffectiveness should be stressed in view of the *seepage of gas odors* from disconnected utilities and piping which may persist for many months. The most satisfactory way to evaluate the clinical effects of the gas range on the health of a chronically sick person is either to remove the stove or the patient, temporarily, and then note the effects of reexposure. If the patient is removed it is essential that he remain *chemically unexposed* while away; that such kitchen contaminants as bleaches, ammonia, plastics, detergents, et cetera, be removed from the room, and upon returning, that the patient remain for two hours in the kitchen before entering other parts of the house. Even then, symptoms may not be evident until during or following the first baking day when there is a heavy gas exposure.

The gas refrigerator, especially if installed in a small tight kitchen, is also a major cause of indoor chemical air pollution. If there is a double installation, both the gas stove and the gas refrigerator should be removed concurrently and replaced singly. The same holds for gas driers.

Perhaps the most pernicious single gas-burning device is the unvented gas-burning room wall heater, used so frequently in the Southwest. In the writer's experience, this installation is one of the chief reasons for the *perpetuation* of chronic symptoms, especially asthma, arthritis and mental syndromes, in persons migrating to that area for their health. Although unvented devices in the middle of the room are worse than vented wall units, neither is to be condoned—either therapeutically or prophylactically.

Fresh Paint and Varnish

Evaporating paint, varnish and other solvent exposures have long been recognized as precipitating factors in bronchial asthma and other allergic-type responses, including more generalized effects. Fortunately, most susceptible persons are aware of the ability of such exposures to induce reactions because of their intermittent dosages. There seems to be little difference between the effects of turpentine and mineral spirits except that some individuals may be more susceptible to one. Indoor painting is best done in summer months, but irrespective of the time of year, victims of this illness should evacuate the premises during and for several days following any type of painting or varnishing in the home.

Casein and alkyd based paints are the most satisfactory substitutes, but the highly susceptible person cannot expect a nil effect from the use of so-called non-odorous paints in closed quarters. Rubber based paints are *not* to be used. Although the odor at the time of application may not be extreme, the persistence of this odor for many months may be responsible for perpetuating chronic effects.

Cements and Other Adhesives

Other major exposures include evaporating solvent constituents of finger nail polish, finger nail polish remover, shoe polishes, paint removers, hinge looseners, adhesives used in model airplanes and other toy fabrications and repairs and also those employed in laying tile or flooring. Some adhesives used in laying tiled surfaces may require several weeks to evaporate fully. Adhesives containing tars used in laying floors are especially troublesome—a hazard that is increased in the presence of heating units in the floor or in the ceilings of downstairs rooms.

Cleaning Fluids and Lighter Fluids

Highly susceptible persons may react to volatile hydrocarbon residues from the mere presence of or from wearing or pressing recently cleaned clothing. In such an event, the work of various cleaners should be compared, inasmuch as the cleaning fluids used by some are apparently of higher grade than others. On-the-floor cleaning of rugs or indoor cleaning of furniture with solvents should be done during a susceptible person's absence and thoroughly evaporated before his return. Home cleaning with solvents should be attempted *outdoors only,* with due regard to wind direction. The materials should be dry and well aired before they are brought into the house. All cleaning and lighter fluids should be stored *outside* the living quarters. Since combustion products used in cigarette and other lighters may precipitate acute attacks in susceptible persons, their presence or use should be barred.

Newsprint

The odor of fresh newsprint constitutes a troublesome exposure for many persons. The mere presence of fresh newspapers in the house may not be tolerated by some, but the most troublesome exposure comes when the newspaper is first opened. Consequently, having someone else first read the paper or placing it in a warm oven for a few minutes, then allowing it to cool before reading may help.

Alcohol

Inhalation of the odor of rubbing alcohol frequently induces acute reactions in the home as well as in physicians' offices. Fumes of alcohol are also encountered in evaporating shellac, brush cleaning preparations and alcohol heaters and lamps. Synthetic alcohol is commonly employed in the manufacture of flavoring extracts and may cause inhalation reactions as it evaporates.

Refrigerants and Spray Containers

The slow escape of refrigerant gases from electric refrigerators and air conditioning equipment may cause chronic symptoms in highly susceptible persons. This is sometimes suggested by a gradually decreasing frosted surface, nearly continuous running of machines or by reactions to stored or frozen foods when the same lot of food, prior to freezing or storage, had not reacted.

The same compressed gas is the most commonly used propellant in spray containers employed in dispensing insecticides, perfumes, hair sprays and other cosmetics. Since many of these *materials* sold in this type container are capable of inducing susceptibility reactions in their own right, these reactions must be differentiated from those attributable to the *propellant* of such devices.

Insecticides

DDT and related chlorinated hydrocarbons, being relatively insoluble in water, are usually dispensed in kerosene or other solvents. Whether the deleterious effects of such mixtures in chemically susceptible persons are due to the *active principles* or the *vehicles* is often difficult to determine. The exceedingly high degree of susceptibility of many persons to such mixtures containing lindane, methoxychlor, DDT, chlordane, malathione or thiocyanates precludes their use as aerosols indoors (29). Rugs are often moth-proofed by the use of DDT in rug shampoos or storage. Although such residues may be largely removed in cleaning, it should be remembered that some cleaning fluids also contain DDT and that rugs and blankets are usually moth-proofed when cleaned, unless otherwise requested.

Toxic insecticides, such as dieldrin, chlordane or pentachlorphenol are often used by professional exterminators for the control of termites and ants. These chemicals should not be used indoors—that is, in the basements or attics of homes of patients known to be susceptible to other chemical exposures. Once these materials are applied, it is impossible to remove them. The only alternative in certain extreme instances has been for susceptible persons to abandon such homes in order to control their chronic symptoms. The odors of slowly evaporating moth balls, cakes and crystals containing naphthalene, paradichlor-benzene and similar materials are also major causes of symptoms in these patients.

Sponge Rubber

Little attention has been paid to the fact that odors arising from sponge rubber pillows, rubber mattresses, rubber upholstery, rubber rug pads, rubber seat cushions, rubber typewriter pads, rubber floor pads, rubber backing of rugs and certain other noise-reducing or shock absorbing installations in the home are major causes of chronic symptoms. Many patients, having substituted sponge rubber for other bedding and upholstery in order to avoid exposure to house dust, find to their dismay that the *rubber odors* are more troublesome. Patients rarely are able to detect this themselves since this cause of chronic symptoms has not been publicized and victims are rarely ever free of such exposures for more than a few hours at a time.

Nevertheless, a highly susceptible person may experience flushing of his face, irritability, and a sense of "stuffiness" or absence of available air upon first entering rooms with rubber rug pads, upholstery or rubber tiled floors. Nocturnal syndrome character- ized by restlessness, insomnia, night sweats and/or residual my- algia and fatigue often suggests the presence of susceptibility to rubber pillows, mattresses or the rubber insulation of electric blankets.

The demonstration of sponge rubber as a major source of in- door chemical air pollution and susceptibility to it are best accomplished after the elimination of gas kitchen utilities. A satisfactory way to determine this is to place *all* sponge rubber items in a single tightly closed room for a week. Provided other exposures bearing on this problem are controlled, chronic symp- toms of a susceptible person are apt to *improve* during this period of avoidance and are also apt to be induced *acutely* soon after breathing the air of this room.

Plastics

The more flexible and odorous a plastic, the more frequently it contributes to indoor chemical air pollution. Bakelite and cellulose acetate products, vinyl floors and surfaces and formica table and counter tops are rarely incriminated, except for an occasional reaction to vinyl and formica as a result of direct skin contact, especially in warm weather. Vinyl and other hard plastic flooring used *in association with* radiant floor heating have been incriminated as causes of chronic symptoms in winter months, but this is believed to be due largely to susceptibility to the *adhesives* rather than to the flooring. Detection is also difficult to unravel if such floors have been *waxed.*

Plastic pillow and mattress cases, upholstery materials, folding doors, shoe bags, hand bags and other cases seem to be the most troublesome offenders. Plastic brushes, combs, powder cases, shoes and other articles of clothing may also be incriminated occasion- ally. Plastic air-conditioning ducts have been determined as a source of airborne odors resulting in reactive symptoms.

If rubber and plastics both are proscribed, one might inquire how the house dust exposure problems are handled. In the writer's experience, the majority of house-dust-sensitive patients are able to sleep on feather pillows if these are laundered several times a year. Dacron pillows are not satisfactory substitutes. The dust problem associated with mattresses, upholstered furniture, rugs and rug pads is handled by frequent cleaning in the patient's absence. Injection therapy with extracts of house dust may be necessary.

Mechanical Devices

Evaporating oil from mechanical devices in the home may also be causes of chronic or acute symptoms in highly susceptible persons. The most commonly encountered illustration is the person reacting to air conditioning equipment, traceable to oil-impregnated glass-wool or fiber filters. In several such instances, the same equipment using *unoiled* filters has been used without reaction. Such persons are usually suspected, erroneously, of being susceptible to chilling or to house dust, but a carefully taken history generally indicates certain air conditioning installations which are *not* troublesome. As previously mentioned, electric or hot water room heating units incorporating a *fan* and *motor* have been found to be relatively common causes of reactions.

Selected instances have been found in which several electrical mechanical devices in small indoor kitchens perpetuated chronic symptoms. For instance, the presence of an electric refrigerator, deep freeze and water cooler in a small room may contribute materially to the air contamination—sufficient to cause symptoms in occasional patients. This problem has been handled by placing these installations in an adjacent room which is entered only occasionally, or by facing such mechanical devices into the kitchen, leaving their backs—and their motors—in an adjacent room.

Automobiles

Since the automobile is becoming increasingly a part of the home—both in respect to the incorporation of the garage in the structure of the house and from the amount of time some persons spend in their cars—it should also be considered here.

Garages should *not* be incorporated into the basements of homes or apartment buildings unless elaborate precautions are taken to prevent the garage odors from rising and fouling the air of living quarters. Whether this can be accomplished is extremely doubtful. Even a direct passageway between the house and an adjacent garage or a common attic may permit the entrance of sufficient car fumes to cause reactions in highly susceptible persons. Careless construction, in which cold air intakes are placed too close to garages or areas fouled by garage odors or other exhausts, often comes to light during routine inspection of homes of highly susceptible persons having unexplained chronic symptoms.

The air of apartment buildings is often contaminated by garage odors from lower floors. This may occur as a result of frequent passage between the garage and the lobby; due to carelessness in construction, or failure to close doors between these two portions of the building. Garage odors often enter elevator shafts from conveniently placed basement openings and foul the halls of upper floors.

Miscellaneous

Inhalation of the odors and fumes of detergents, naphtha containing soaps, ammonia, Chlorox, cleansing powders containing bleaches, window washing compounds, certain silver and brass polishing materials, and burning wax candles may cause chronic or acute symptoms. The mere storage in the home of bleach-containing cleansers has been incriminated. In general, this group of patients have far more tolerance for unscented soaps and cleansers and for abrasives without added bleach.

Highly scented soaps, toilet deodorants and disinfectants—especially pine-scented, phenol-containing or those with pungent chemical odors—are common causes of indoor air pollution to which many individuals are highly susceptible. So-called "air improvers" which depend upon the evaporation of chemical ingredients are also common causes of reaction. The incorporation of phenol and chemicals employed for *extermination* in the paste of wall paper recently has come to light.

Pine exposures, either from Christmas decorations or from burning pine wood in fireplaces, trouble some patients.

Although creosote rarely enters the home except occasionally in medicinals, one susceptible patient was forced to sell his home because of the odors of creosote arising from the close proximity of radiant heating floor units and creosote impregnated floor supports.

The storage of highly scented perfumes and other cosmetics may be sufficient to foul the air of homes.

Odors arising from prolonged use of television and radio sets may foul the air in the vicinity of such devices.

Public Places

Indoor chemical exposures found in public places are much the same as in homes except that the use of deodorants, disinfectants, pine-scented sweeping compounds and spraying for insect control may be encountered even more commonly. Most troublesome of these are the pine-scented or chemical deodorants of public toilets. Acute reactions of patients following such exposures are becoming increasingly common.

Fuel-oil or gas space heaters are also found more often in small shops, stores and restaurants than in homes; these are major causes of *chronic* reactions in workers and *acute* responses in customers. Although the heating facilities of larger buildings, such as schools, factories and office buildings are generally more satisfactory, there are many exceptions to this statement.

Improper school room heating is a major reason for the poor performance of susceptible children and/or their teachers. This frequently gives rise to the hyperactive, inattentive, irritable, tired and day-dreamy child. Even more acute reactions may manifest as *extreme* hyperactivity, flushing of the face, unteachability and the compulsive desires to run and race aimlessly. A sleepy mathematics teacher in a room directly above the school cafeteria, from which gas stove odors arose through an open stairwell, improved greatly in his health and performance when transferred to a more distant room. *Indoor chemical air pollution of schools* as a contributing cause of poor scholastic performance of susceptible children and the dopiness and confusion of susceptible teachers *is rarely diagnosed correctly!* Other susceptible teachers among the writer's patients have been helped by being transferred from classrooms directly over the furnace room or in close proximity to the indoor swimming pool and shops, thus being spared the odors arising therefrom. The problem presented by indoor air pollution is sufficiently acute to warrant the transfer of certain highly susceptible students and teachers to more satisfactorily located, constructed, equipped, heated and ventilated schools. Exposure to tobacco smoke in college classrooms also is a major problem.

Chemical indoor air pollution in offices differs from that in homes. There are exposures to carbon paper, inks, mimeographing and duplicating devices, rubber cement, typewriters, typewriter pads, perfumes worn by women employes; also certain occupational hazards at times as a result of the office being adjacent to or sharing common heating and ventilating equipment with shops and warehouses. Many individuals susceptible to chemical exposures are also highly susceptible to tobacco smoke— an exposure that often reaches heavy concentrations in many offices.

Chemical air contamination of hospitals is contributed to by the gas utilities of laboratories and kitchens; chemical deodorants, disinfectants and cleansers; the odors of ether and other volatile anesthetics blown off by recently operated patients; odors arising from the use of certain drugs; the odors from rubbing alcohol; perfumes worn by hospital personnel and visitors; rubber draw sheets and other rubber and plastic bedding and furniture.

Chemical air pollution of churches centers about the gas utilities in the kitchens, the burning of wax candles and incense, perfumes and the odors of recently stored furs and outer clothing.

Hotel exposures are essentially the same as those in homes and apartment buildings. The most troublesome air contaminants are the pine and chemically scented toilet deodorants, sponge rubber and plastic bedding and furniture.

The air of supermarkets and other retail grocery stores is frequently fouled by the odors of insecticide sprays, disinfectants, deodorants, and pine or chemically scented cleaning compounds The practice of spraying disinfectants over and around fruit and vegetable counters is deplored, both on the basis of contamination of air and of produce.

Indoor chemical air pollution of schools, churches, hospitals and other public places reflects the extent of *outdoor* chemical air contamination of the general area as well as pollutants arising from adjacent parking lots. This may be from the volatility of the cars or from the extensive asphalt surfaces of such areas.

Although *occupational* exposures are beyond the scope of this presentation, the most troublesome fumes and odors for the group of patients under consideration are evaporating solvents and their combustion products; the odors of rubber, plastic, resins, detergents, cutting and lubricating oils, sulfur, chlorine and other halogens. The interested reader is referred to reviews bearing on the question of individual susceptibility to occupational exposures (30-31).

B. OUTDOOR CHEMICAL AIR CONTAMINATION
Outdoor Chemical Air Pollution in Chicago

In general, outdoor chemical air pollution of metropolitan industrial regions is accentuated on quiet, humid, foggy or rainy days. This type of weather is apt to be more common in winter and progressively less so in spring, fall and summer. However, summertime is by no means a period free of air contamination. Automotive traffic is not only greater but a given vehicle contaminates more air in hot weather because of the increased volatility of its exhausts, engine odors and plastic and rubber installations.

Aside from the peculiarities of geography and weather previously mentioned, the problem of outdoor chemical air pollution presented by Chicago may be taken as an *example* of other large metropolitan areas. This city contains four major foci of outdoor chemical air pollution, important in the production and perpetuation of chronic symptoms in susceptible persons. The greatest of these localized sources, as judged by the clinical response of susceptible persons, is the petroleum refinery area at the extreme northern border of Illinois and Indiana. Another rapidly growing and similar refinery focus is in the area adjoining the ship canal southwest of Chicago. Another more diffuse focus centers about a large paint manufacturing plant on the south side of the city, located near several heavy industries. The fourth area, even more diffuse, centers in the Loop. Automotive and railroad traffic odors are its major contributors. Traffic-contaminated expressways and dieselized railroads extend peripherally in spoke-like fashion.

Depending upon the direction and strength of the wind and certain other weather conditions, these foci frequently overlap, or the contaminated blanket of air overlying them is pushed in one direction or another. As previously mentioned, the concentration of these three manufacturing and refinery regions to the south, gives this portion of the city a relatively more constant atmospheric pollution than occurs in other areas.

Also, there are important *vertical* limitations of outdoor air pollution in this area. Downtown air pollution is worse at street level and in basements of downtown stores, although there appears to be little difference as far as the first few floors are concerned. Atmospheric contamination as a major factor in the production of symptoms in the susceptible, ordinarily is not troublesome above the twentieth floor of Loop buildings. Although present in subways, air contamination there is not as excessive as might be expected because of the air turbulence.

The problem of outdoor chemical air pollution in this area is illustrated by the following case. An architect with a history of advanced susceptibility to diverse chemical exposures, as manifested by rhinitis, coughing, headache, fatigue, mental confusion and intermittent bouts of depression, lived in the first suburb west of Chicago. He commuted daily to the center of the city and for a full year kept a *log* on his *symptoms,* correlating them with *weather conditions.* The factors of *indoor* chemical air contamination and other chemical exposures had been limited as far as possible by a change of residence—an electrically equipped, hot-water-heated home having a detached garage; all sponge rubber, odorous plastics and other indoor sources of contamination had been eliminated. He maintained a diet and water supply known to be relatively uncontaminated by chemicals and took no drugs. His home was in a residential area several blocks from industrial installations, railroads or expressways.

In general, he remained more comfortable in his home than in his downtown office, even though storage of blue prints and other sources of air contaminants had been removed. But, significantly, even with the ideal home conditions, he remained symptom-free *only* when the wind was blowing from the west, northwest and north. Invariably, he had a recurrence of symptoms in association with an east wind, which brought the Chicago air contaminants, and even more so with a southeast wind, bringing fumes from the industrialized refinery section. Even winds from the south and southwest were troublesome, yet this patient had no trouble with winds from any direction if blowing at the rate of *15 or more miles per hour*. The *most troublesome* were the "drift" winds from the southeast which blow between three and seven miles per hour. This holds true for all patients susceptible to chemicals and reacting to outdoor air contaminants in this area.

This patient's *bad days* for the entire year not only checked with these weather conditions but also correlated with visability as measured by the U. S. Weather Bureau.

There has been a long-standing need for more precise measurements of chemical air contaminants. Lacking such determinations, visability—as measured by the distance one is able to see spaced lights—appears to be the best over-all indicator, as the problem has been studied clinically in this region.

To illustrate the carrying capacity of drift winds, refinery odors arising from extreme Northwestern Indiana may carry across the tip of Lake Michigan and cause impaired visability and acute symptoms along the North Shore, 75 miles distant. Another similar drift wind at five miles per hour from the south-southwest carried detectable refinery odors from the Joliet region to Waukegan. Four highly susceptible patients in a line corresponding to a "cigar-shaped" shaded area of a fallout map were simultaneously *acutely ill* between 40 and 75 miles from the source of this contamination. Although these are unusual circumstances, it may be said conservatively that there is no residential area within a 50 miles radius of the center of Chicago which is consistently *free* from air contaminants arising from the city and environs. It should be noted that this statement considers only one aspect of the outdoor air contamination problem. Certain other chemical exposures are accentuated in suburban areas, as will be described.

Engine Exhausts

General Considerations

From attempts to evaluate the clinical effects of motor exhausts on susceptible persons, the most immediate and acute reactions seem to result from *diesel* truck, bus, tractor, train and boat exhausts. The next most common cause of acute reactions are the odorous and/or bluish-colored exhausts arising from *any* motor vehicle. This general type of exhaust characterizes operating *diesel* engines at *all* times; otherwise, it seems to arise principally from non-diesel engines in *poor mechanical adjustment* or repair and when mechanically satisfactory engines are *decelerating;* also when *first started in cold weather.* Diesel and non-diesel exhausts, arising from a relatively incomplete combustion of fuels, are especially noxious in precipitating acute intermittent reactions in susceptible persons. However, exhausts of gasoline-burning engines operating at maintenance speed, in view of their larger number, are probably greater sources of metropolitan air pollution and chronic symptoms.

Air contamination of major cities attributable to motor exhausts is generally heaviest in the central business and industrial districts. Spokes of contaminated air not only radiate peripherally to the open country, following the course of railroads, truck routes, bus lines, expressways and other major traffic arterials, but also criss-cross such a metropolitan area. Foci of relatively greater air pollution, resulting from deceleration, occur at train stations and traffic stops. Although wind direction, velocity and turbulence determine the degree of contamination at any given point, the fact remains that the closer a susceptible person lives to a city's central area, its major routes and "stop" intersections, the greater his *exhaust exposures.* This statement is based on observation of the clinical effects on patients in many families advised to move from homes adjacent or near diesel railroads, truck or bus lines, expressways and stop-light corners. Some highly susceptible individuals may have their chronic illness *perpetuated* from such exposures when living within three city blocks of major expressways.

In general, one may assume that if he is able to hear the *roar* of automotive traffic that he may also be reacting to the *fumes* of it, irrespective of whether he may be able to *detect* their odors. Conversely, the less the roar, the less the odor, since both tend to be carried by the same air movements.

Although directions for avoiding exposures to traffic odors will be outlined later, the basis for such recommendations will be discussed forthwith.

Diesel Exhausts

Exposure of passengers on diesel trains to chemical fumes arising from the engine are greatest at points of entrance and exit from such trains. This is especially true of underground or covered stations in which passengers are forced to walk past a line of "purring" locomotives to reach their coach or the station exit. Train sheds designed for steam locomotives, having overhead apertures for carrying off smoke, are unsatisfactory for diesel engines since these exhausts are relatively heavier than air and tend to settle. Some highly susceptible patients become acutely ill each time they attempt to run such a gauntlet. Other than this, passengers are apt to have less exposure to odors from riding on diesel propelled trains than when traveling the same distance during rush hours by bus or automobile, though of course there is considerable variation in the amount of exposure in different trains. When all common modes of transportation at ground level are considered, the electric elevated train, followed by the electric subway train, seems to be associated with the least pollution. Despite the tendency of certain traffic odors to settle in low places, air turbulence and ventilation in subways usually dissipate most of the odors that collect there.

Due to the tendency of a moving vehicle to suck in its own exhausts through cracks and open windows, riders sitting in the rear of rear-engine diesel buses are more exposed to exhaust than those sitting or standing in front. This exposure is increased if favored by wind direction. The tendency for buses to follow each other closely also favors the entrance of exhaust of the lead bus into the passenger compartment of the following vehicle. Although this danger exists for any type of motor vehicle, it is especially marked in diesel buses and trucks. Despite the exhausts of propane-fueled buses causing far less acute reactions, these exhausts also are capable of producing identical reactions in susceptible persons if exposure is sufficiently great.

Passengers often develop headaches or other reactions during or following bus trips, without suspecting exhaust exposures. These effects usually are cumulative, often manifesting only after a certain mileage or time in the bus. In less susceptible persons they may manifest only when riding in vehicles in poor mechanical repair or only when the rear windows are open. Localized reactions associated with such exposures are more often noted than the equally important *constitutional manifestations*. For instance, the fatigue associated with riding the bus downtown and shopping is frequently out of proportion to the actual activity involved.

One particularly instructive patient developed fatigue and headache following each injection of house dust extract, despite the elimination of chemical preservatives in the injected material and repeated reductions in dosage. The same reaction occurred after an injection of preservative-free normal saline, and again after the jab of a *dry* needle. Finally, after the same reaction occurred when the patient was turned back at the door *without receiving any injection,* the bus transportation was suspected. It was then learned that fatigue and headache did not occur when the trip was made by *elevated train* but invariably occurred following the trip by bus.

Another patient manifested abdominal cramps and diarrhea after riding a few blocks in a diesel bus, but was able to ride several miles in a propane fueled bus before the onset of similar symptoms. Sleepiness and mental confusion on bus trips is also a common manifestation of reactions in the chemically susceptible person.

Gasoline Exhausts

Automobile passengers are far less exposed to exhausts when riding in the *front seat*. Rear seat fume exposures are accentuated when rear side windows are open, especially so if the rear gate window of a station wagon is open. Eddy currents induced by the relative vacuum immediately behind a vehicle traveling above a certain critical rate of speed are extraordinarily effective in fouling the air in rear seats. Although the recent tendency of manufacturers to direct the exhausts of station wagons to the side is helpful, insucking of a station wagon's own exhaust remains a hazardous exposure.

Not only are susceptible passengers exposed to the exhausts of their own car and others in heavy traffic, but interior appointments in automobiles are also major sources of odors causing reactions in this group of patients. Rubber floor coverings, plastic upholstery, and sponge rubber cushions and padding are associated with reactions in susceptible persons in direct proportion to their odors. These sources usually are incriminated in the order named. Although a new automobile is usually more odorous in these respects than the same car after a period of use, the ability of these odors to induce reactions in susceptible persons is never entirely lost. In view of the marked differences between makes of cars as well as between models of the same manufacturer, a person with this illness should shop around until finding a new or used car in which he can ride in the open country comfortably. The "open country" is stipulated, for under these circumstances he is less apt to react to odors arising from *outside* his own vehicle.

In the writer's experience in supervising the purchase of automobiles for several extremely susceptible persons, this usually means *carpeting* instead of rubber floor coverings and *leather* or *nylon* upholstery and top interiors. Nylon, however, is not entirely safe, as it may cause reactions as a result of direct contact though not by inhalation. This will be discussed under a later heading.

Occasionally the odors arising from leaking anti-freeze, leaking brake fluids, heaters and rubber tires may be associated with similar reactions. Thus far, at least, plastic steering wheels and other hard plastics of the interiors of automobiles have not been incriminated as causes of inhalant reactions.

Hazardous Manifestations Due to Traffic Odors

A driver's impaired ability to operate a motor vehicle when either in chronic or acute reactions from chemical odors or fumes to which he is susceptible is *one of the most serious aspects of this medical problem.* Since chronic reactions are the slyest to detect, these will be considered first. Rhinitis, coughing, asthma, gastrointestinal and other localized symptoms or such general effects as headaches, myalgia or arthralgia are probably the most common. Although these symptoms are distractive and have a considerable nuisance value, car sickness (nausea, vomiting with or without dizziness and headache) is probably the most common. *Car* sickness should not be confused with *motion* sickness. It is of interest that this common manifestation of susceptibility to chemical odors and fumes is generally more pronounced in congested traffic than open country driving. Many victims of car sickness have learned empirically that they are less ill in the front than rear seats; some tolerate certain cars better than others in making an identical trip; several have been able to withstand the motion of elevated or cross-country electric trains without developing symptoms.

Potentially the most dangerous chronic reaction to the inhalation of odors and fumes is the gradual onset of fatigue and *overpowering sleepiness.* As this also usually occurs after several hours of exposure, it is exceedingly difficult—if not impossible—to differentiate from physical fatigue or even so-called driver hypnosis. Fatigue of the type occurring in these reactions is characterized by dopiness (impairment of memory, attention, concentration and comprehension) as well as irritability (6,18). Persons in such reactions tend to under-react in their ability to make quick decisions and to act on them. But they over-react in the sense that they tend to be easily annoyed by other persons and events. The latter sometimes manifests as extreme anger which, in a confused driver, may be directed toward another driver or car. Although these cutbacks in acuity of perception, association and tolerance for the mistakes of others are serious enough, the *greatest single hazard* is the tendency for drivers suffering reactions to chemical additives and contaminants of air or food—or foods *per se*— to doze off at the wheel.

Whereas chronic reactions gradually impair perceptual and associative cerebral functions, acute reactions—usually resulting from more massive exposures—are apt to manifest initially as impairment of *motor function* and *proprioception*. Irritability may be associated with either. The earliest symptoms of an acute reaction may consist of "nervousness," tenseness, blurring of vision and lesser degrees of muscular incoordination. Although symptoms may not develop beyond this stage, it often progresses to general clumsiness characterized by over-reaching, under-reaching and ataxia suggestive of drunkenness. These drunk-like reactions also resemble alcoholic inebriation in that the reactor often presents a ruddy complexion, hoarseness, hyperactivity, and both a general tendency to *underestimate* the *degree of reaction* and to *overestimate the ability to drive.*

This parallelism may be carried even farther. The alcohol-inebriated person cannot tell the location of his feet unless looking at them. Drivers in this stage of chemically induced cerebral reactions are inaccurate in gauging the force applied to the accelerator or brake—unless they look—and this is *even more hazardous*. Certain rapidly advancing acute reactions in the extremely susceptible (as illustrated in the foregoing case reports) may lead to loss of consciousness or convulsive seizures. However, the majority of acute responses come on sufficiently gradually that a person, aware of reacting in this manner, usually has time to protect himself before such a termination. Slowly progressing acute reactions taper off at any given level, first merging with and then being superseded by a corresponding level of more delayed chronic symptoms, as previously described.

Both *chronic* effects resulting from small cumulative exposures over an extended period of time and more *acute* reactions associated with greater exposures are believed to be responsible for a portion of the so-called "irreducible" human error in traffic accidents. Individuals with a known propensity for developing reactions of this type should drive less congested routes or always be accompanied by another person in the front seat who is capable of assuming control of the car in such an event. Another relatively under-emphasized danger in the case of a solitary driver finding himself slipping into a severe reaction in his tendency to *infract any traffic custom,* rule or regulation hindering his escape from such a threatening situation before it overwhelms him. This is especially apt to occur in the lone driver caught behind a diesel vehicle or one in poor mechanical repair which is trailing a blue flume. This type of driving behavior on the part of a chemically susceptible person may so startle other drivers and pedestrians in the vicinity that a victim's zeal to flee from a bad situation leads to a worse one—an accident. These factors explain many traffic accidents which are reported merely as caused by the driver "going to sleep at the wheel."

What has been said about chronically dopey and/or acutely incoordinated driver's reaction to chemical additives and contaminants holds equally well for pedestrians wading through a ground-level blanket of urban smog. Indeed, this illness is so common that a driver can never assume a normal degree of perception and awareness of danger on a pedestrian's part nor his expected agility to escape from a threatening situation. The writer has seen patients so confused during reactions to chemical additives and contaminants, as well as to foods *per se,* that they changed their minds about crossing a street, reversing their course in the middle of it!

The chemically susceptible driver should also take particular care in refueling his car. Since most gasoline stations have multiple pumps approachable from various directions, after appraising the wind direction, he should drive into the station in a head-wind—as if landing an airplane. Then, after giving his instructions, he should either close the windows and remain inside or step away from the car as the tank is filled. The highly susceptible should not enter garages, especially body and paint shops. Certain individuals with unusually severe reaction potentialities should carry oxygen equipment in their cars at all times for use in case of emergencies. A more convenient and useful device is a cannister from a civilian gas mask containing activated carbon and equipped with Tygon* plastic tubing. By breathing through this home-made device, shown in Figure I, which is equipped with an exhale valve in the tubing a few inches from the mouth aperture, one may pass through tunnels, follow diesel trucks or buses in traffic or be subjected to massive airborne chemical exposures with impunity.

---

* A special plastic manufactured for the food industry which is odorless and has been tolerated by these patients.

Fig. 1. Home-made mask, employing a Civilian Defense activated carbon cannister and Tygon tubing, for the removal of airborne chemical odors and fumes.

Fogging for Insect Abatement and Weed Control

A major factor contributing to outdoor air contamination of areas not generally fouled otherwise is the increasing practice of fogging for insect control near urban centers. Persons known to be intolerant to various chemical exposures associated with city living often move to the suburban country side for their health, only to be "abated" without warning in the middle of the night! Having retired with bedroom windows open, a susceptible person's first warning of the presence of the municipally financed mosquito abatement spray rig may be a strangling cough or even an epileptiform seizure. The writer has been called out at night on several different occasions to resuscitate such patients. Susceptible persons protect themselves from abatement programs variously. Some have requested the local agency to give them advance notice when their area is to be treated so they may choose between fleeing the region or enclosing themselves in their own homes. Some have moved farther into the country, but this usually fails. Either a new agency is formed in this region; they run into trouble with farmers spraying for weed control, or foresters spraying for insect pests. A few have actually returned to the most livable part of the city from which they moved, finding its hazards less disturbing than the current indiscriminate spraying of the countryside.

Even while driving in the country, one may suddenly encounter roadside weed control spraying. The highly susceptible person is well advised to stop, turn around and escape as rapidly as possible. An alternate move is to close his car windows and breathe through his activated carbon cannister. Even driving along a recently sprayed roadside or railroad right-of-way or through a country area immediately after spraying for weed or insect control may precipitate reactions.

Tar Roofing and Road Construction

Encountering a fuming tar trailer used in roofing and road construction or a recently tarred road also provides this type patient with a similar emergency. This should be handled as above described. When the roof, alley, road or parking lot near one's home is being tarred, victims of this illness are advised to flee for a week or more. But upon returning and for at least a year following, during direct sun exposure these areas remain a major source of both outdoor and indoor air contamination.

Miscellaneous Exposures

One occasionally encounters an odorous smudge from burning of old automobile tires, creosoted railroad ties or other chemically impregnated wood. The odors of such materials or those from burning dumps may constitute a major traffic hazard when occurring in close proximity to a traffic arterial. The fumes from burning paraffin-coated milk cartons and waxed food wrappers, in communities where dry garbage is incinerated locally, contributes to air pollution in general and to the ill health of susceptible persons. Similar reactions sometimes follow burning of oil impregnated rags or other oily or chemically treated household debris.

Part IV

CHEMICAL CONTAMINATION
OF INGESTANTS

A. FOOD ADDITIVES AND CONTAMINANTS

Introduction

A FOOD ADDITIVE is any chemical substance that makes its way into a food. There are certain intentional additives whose use in given amounts is approved by law, as well as certain other chemical substances which enter the food supply incidentally. The latter might also be referred to as chemical contaminants. Both exert important clinical effects, as will be pointed out. Since these two uses cannot always be differentiated, the entire subject of man made chemicals entering the food supply will be referred to by the designation, chemical additives and contaminants.

Susceptibility to chemical additives and contaminants of the diet has long been confused with specific susceptibility to foods as such (8). This confusion should have been expected, since both apparently involve adaptation processes; both commonly coexist in the same individual; manifest in similar symptoms and are exceedingly difficult to separate. In fact, separation did not occur until reliable sources of relatively non-contaminated food became available for test purposes. Only then did it become evident that at least certain patients, originally thought to have been sensitive to certain *foods,* turned out to have a major *chemical food contamination* problem. Others were found to be primarily food sensitive but with slight, if any, demonstrable susceptibility to chemical additives and contaminants of the diet.

The separation of these two closely related conditions also provided answers to several previously baffling observations—data that at times had been used to discredit the existence of specific food susceptibility. Most troublesome to explain was the inconsistency of a given food to induce clinical reactions in patients known to have been highly susceptible to that food when the same item from different sources was fed under otherwise identical conditions of testing. Rowe's observations of the frequency of multiple fruit sensitization—at variance with the tendency for involvement of the diet to follow botanical groupings (23)—and the apparent accentuation of food allergy during winter months (32) also remained unexplained.

It should be emphasized that the observations to be reported— differentiating *reactions from chemical additives and contaminants of foods* from *susceptibility to foods per se*—should be made with a full understanding of the dynamic nature of both processes. Although the nature of the chemical problem is described herewith, the reader is referred to other sources for descriptions of food susceptibility or food allergy (8,13,16). Test procedures, in both instances, should be carried out during nonadapted phases of reaction, as described earlier in this article.

Observations of a physician-patient, known to have been highly susceptible to apples and peaches, initiated this interest. Although he developed a headache each time he ate commercially available peaches or apples, he found that he was able to eat these homegrown *unsprayed* fruits with impunity. These observations remained unexplained until interpreted on the basis of the cultural and technological contamination of these foods, on the one hand, and this patient's susceptibility to numerous chemical exposures, on the other. As these leads were pursued and chemically uncontaminated foods became available for test purposes, these inconsistencies in the results of repeated individual food ingestion tests were explained. Moreover, certain of these patients appeared to react definitely to these commercially available and relatively contaminated foods during *winter months* when concomitantly exposed to heavy concentrations of indoor chemical air pollution.

Some of these patients also remained chronically ill in Chicago at any time of the year—apparently the result of exposure to *outdoor chemical air pollution*—since they improved in rural areas, provided the major sources of chemical contaminants of their living quarters, diet and water supplies had been controlled. In others, the additional effects of pollens, spores, dusts and seasonal chemical exposures superimposed other reaction patterns.

These points illustrate the multiplicity of inter-relationship of impinging exposures as far as an afflicted individual is concerned. Presentation of the subject unfortunately necessitates first an arbitrary division limited to food contaminants and subdivisions of that subject.

Spray Residues

So-called Multiple Fruit Sensitization

Three patients, clinically susceptible to multiple chemical exposures, were selected for a preliminary study. After eating peaches they manifested severe urticaria, asthma and headache, respectively. Commercial peaches purchased on the market and similar ones from an abandoned orchard were employed as unknowns. All three reacted to the ingestion of the commercial fruit but failed to react to the technologically uncontaminated peaches (33).

The following season, four lots of peaches were tested in like manner in 15 additional subjects. Although the same type of peach was used in all tests, their technology differed as follows: 1) Peaches picked from trees of an abandoned orchard, having received no sprays, fungicidal treatment or fertilization for the previous three years. 2) Same as the above except that the fruit had been manually dusted with sulfur as a fungicidal measure. 3) Peaches from one of the University of Illinois Department of Horticulture plots which had received the recommended spray schedules using DDT and Dieldrin. 4) Peaches from the same source sprayed with Parathione and Dieldrin.*

For several days prior to each blind ingestion test, all subjects had been avoiding both peaches and chemical exposures to which they had been known to be susceptible. Three of the 15 subjects were made acutely ill following the ingestion of chemically *uncontaminated* peaches. In contrast to this small group, a larger number of the others reacted to both the *sulfured* and the *sprayed* peaches.

---

* Furnished through the courtesy of Dr. George Decker, Department of Entomology.

The severity of these reactions in some instances dissuaded them from continuing with the battery of blind ingestion tests. Because of this, the series was never completed. But as several who were negative to the controls reacted to each type of contamination, it may be said that there was something about both the sulfured peaches and those treated with insecticide-solvent mixtures that precipitated *acute* reactions. There were no apparent differences in the degree or severity of reactions between the two types of sprayed peaches; each person who had been tested to both sprayed lots reacted to both. Whether the active ingredient of the spray or the oil vehicle was responsible for the reactions was not determined.

From subsequent observations in many other similar patients, the presence of clinical reactions to several commercially available fruits—irrespective of their botanical groupings—suggests the presence of susceptibility to a common technology associated with *fruit culture* rather than a *multiple specific food allergy.* The greater the background of susceptibility to chemical contaminants in a given case, the more likely this interpretation, although multiple fruit sensitization, in the absence of demonstrable susceptibility to the chemical environment, may occur. It is of special interest that the majority who had been avoiding numerous fruits for many years have since been able to eat most of the previously suspected chemically less-contaminated fruits.

In general, the scope of this so-called "multiple fruit sensitivity" is variable from patient to patient, being the more inclusive in those with the greatest degree of susceptibility to *chemical* exposures. Peaches, apples and cherries seem to be the most commonly contaminated as well as heaviest in their contamination. Although the total number of spraying applications varies with rainfall and other conditions, peaches, apples and cherries may be sprayed between 10 and 15 times per season. Recommended spray schedules start with blossoming and end only a few weeks prior to harvesting. The fact remains, however, that most commercially produced fruits in the United States are *copiously sprayed,* some are dusted with sulfur, some fumigated or otherwise contaminated in growth or handling, as will be described. Since the technology of a given fruit may involve several possible chemical contaminations, it often requires considerable experimentation to be certain that a *given additive* is the *cause* of a *given reaction.*

Once a fruit has been sprayed with a combination of chlorinated hydrocarbons and kerosene or some other chemically derived insecticide-solvent mixture, *there is no known way of removing such spray residues.* Since a growing or stored fruit has a continuous exchange of air between it and its surroundings, the spray ingredients apparently become *incorporated into the pulp of the fruit.* Washing, rubbing, peeling, cooking or combinations of these processes do not eliminate spray residues, as judged by the ability of fruits so contaminated to precipitate acute reactions when ingested as unknowns by highly susceptible persons. Nevertheless, there is a group of lesser susceptible persons who, when *avoiding* other chemical exposures, may be able to eat commercially available *stewed* fruits although unable to eat the same lot of *fresh* fruit. Since these spray residues are at least partially volatile, this may account for the common observation that stewed fruits seem to be better tolerated by some individuals than the same fruits in their raw state. In keeping with this view is the fact that *inhalation of the odors of chemically contaminated* stewing fruits and vegetables have precipitated clinical reactions in some, though cooking odors of the same items *not so contaminated* have been tolerated.

However, it bears reemphasis that even highly susceptible persons eating a general diet rarely suspect the daily ingestion of fruits containing the usual spray residues. These conditions simply tend to perpetuate chronic symptoms. Only occasionally—when the intake of chemical contaminants may be excessively high—does such a dose break through this level of chronic symptoms so as to induce an acute obvious reaction.

So-called Multiple Vegetable Sensitivity

Individuals susceptible to various other chemical exposures often are unable to eat cabbage, broccoli, cauliflower, celery, lettuce, spinach, beet greens and certain other leafy vegetables belonging to various botanical families. Several such patients have been found susceptible to *sprayed* vegetables but not to the same vegetables *unsprayed*. Of this group, the members of the cabbage family seem to be the most copiously contaminated. Whereas all cooks were formerly alerted to the presence of cabbage worms on broccoli, the writer has not known of anyone who uses commercially available vegetables encountering worms on broccoli during the past decade.

Other practices contributing to the spray contamination of foods is the *indiscriminate spraying of fruit and vegetable counters* in retail markets. This apparently is done to control fruit flies. Susceptible persons usually start to cough, wheeze, or manifest some other evidence of reaction when in this area of markets. Admittedly, these reactions are difficult to differentiate from those attributable to the evaporation of previously applied spray-solvent mixtures as well as those from the inhalation of deodorants, disinfectants and cleaners used in the markets. The fact that the majority of such reactions occur in the vicinity of the produce counters and the fact that spraying of such areas is known to be a common practice suggests this exposure as the predominant one.

Spray Residues and Other Contaminants of Meat and Poultry

The fat of certain commercially available meat, especially lamb, beef and some poultry, is apparently contaminated chemically. This is judged by the ability of such fats to induce symptoms in patients highly susceptible to certain other chemical exposures. The major sources of this contamination appear to be *chlorinated hydrocarbon sprays* and/or their vehicles, believed to occur as a result of feeding *sprayed forage* and/or the common practice of *spraying herds for insect control*.

As might be expected, there are considerable variations in the effects of different sources of these meats. In the majority of instances, these reactions may be avoided or greatly reduced by cutting off *all fat* prior to cooking. Nevertheless, a few patients, otherwise avoiding sources of chemical exposures, still react to beef or lamb from which the fat had been removed as far as possible, but are able to eat the same meat known not to have been chemically contaminated. Others, as might be expected, are actually susceptible to one of these foods per se, as judged by the ability of samples, known to have been relatively *uncontaminated chemically,* to induce acute test effects. The possibility that patients may be reacting to *other* chemical additives and contaminants of meat and fowl has not been excluded. These will be discussed later.

Fumigant Residues

Several patients known to be susceptible to one or more related chemical exposures have been *able* to eat dates known to have been relatively uncontaminated chemically but *unable* to eat dates from the *same grove* known to have been fumigated with methyl bromide. It is not generally known that *Federal regulations* demand that dates be fumigated in this manner before entering interstate commerce. However, it is of particular interest—in view of the well known laxative effect of *dates* and *figs*—that these fruits, relatively free of chemical contaminants, may generally be taken in one- or two-pound lots *without* inducing laxative effects. These observations suggest that the laxative action of certain commercially available fruits, especially dates and figs, lies in their *mandatory additives* rather than in the fruits *per se.* Exception to this statement might include those persons with a specific susceptibility to uncontaminated sources and manifesting gastrointestinal responses to their ingestion. It should be emphasized that the total effects of commercially available dates, figs and fruits handled similarly is difficult to evaluate because of the common practice of spraying and other techniques involving additional additives.

Commercially available shelled nuts also commonly precipitate acute reactions in some chemically susceptible patients otherwise avoiding major chemical exposures, whereas the same freshly shelled nuts are often taken with impunity—in the absence of true susceptibility to these uncontaminated foods *per se.*

The same statement holds for commercially available dried peas, beans and lentils, as contrasted to the response of the same patients to those known to have escaped fumigation. Dried fruits are also apt to be fumigated; but since they are also *apt to have been sprayed* and *may have been sulfured,* no attempt has been made as yet to sort out the sources of reactions commonly occurring in chemically susceptible persons. These comments point up the fact that simply buying dried fruits advertised as *unsulfured* does not insure one of an *uncontaminated* source of supply, since the majority of samples also have been sprayed and fumigated!

During the past year ingestion tests have been performed with commercially available sources of wheat and corn; also with samples of these grains grown in the absence of chemical fertilization and additives. Indeed, the farm on which the samples were grown had not had commercially available fertilizers used on it for the past 30 years, and the grains were ground in a stone mill used only for materials originating on this farm.

When parallel ingestion tests were performed with these materials of known cultural and technological pedigree and with unenriched commercially available wheat and with corn meal, a relatively greater number of chemically susceptible patients reacted to the commercial materials. In all instances, these materials were cooked in spring water and salted to taste.

Also, a greater number reacted to commercial corn meal than to commercial cracked wheat cereal, although the incidence of sensitivity to these two cereal grains is approximately the same (13). This difference may be attributable to the *sulfur treatment* of corn products, which will be discussed later, although both commercially available supplies may have been fumigated in storage.

Bleaches

Bleaching agents (oxides of nitrogen, chlorine and benzoyl peroxide) employed in whitening flour have not been separated from other potential sources of chemical contamination of wheat. Clinical responses attributable to eating of white bread cannot be interpreted as incriminating bleached flour because of the host of *other additives* of *chemical origin* entering the current manufacture of bread.

Sulfur

It is also difficult to evaluate clinical effects apparently arising from the treatment of foods with sulfur because of the multiplicity of other possible contaminants as well as existence of susceptibility to the uncontaminated food *per se.* Nevertheless, the several times that this has been attempted in individuals having aspects of the chemical problem, leaves the impression that *sulfur is a major chemical contaminant* of the food supply.

In the course of performing ingestion tests with peaches dusted with sulfur but otherwise uncontaminated, several test subjects reacted acutely to the sulfured peaches. The most acute reaction occurred in a woman who had failed to react to uncontaminated peaches. Twenty minutes following the ingestion of a sulfured peach she complained of nervousness and tenseness with alternating chilling and sweating sensations. She became nauseated at 30 minutes; vomited a part of the peach at 35 minutes. At 40 minutes she remained cold, clammy, pale and depressed. Despite pumping her stomach contents, she continued to manifest severe abdominal cramps, residual aching, fatigue and depression for the remainder of the day.

A few patients have inquired why they were unable to eat French fried potatoes in restaurants, whereas home French fried potatoes were taken without trouble. Investigation revealed the almost universal practice of larger restaurants to purchase peeled and sliced potatoes for French frying which had been dipped in a *solution of sulfur dioxide* as an anti-browning measure. The same routine may be employed in the manufacture of potato chips and in handling freshly cut apples and peaches.

Dried fruits are commonly treated with sulfur, as previously mentioned. Some *fresh* fruits and vegetables, notably asparagus, are blanched with solutions containing sulfur dioxide.

The processing of corn begins with soaking of the whole kernels in sulfur dioxide solution. Although this practice avoids fermentation while the physical parts of the kernels are separated, it apparently imparts a sulfur contamination to all manufactured corn products. These include cornstarch, corn flour, corn sugar (dextrose and glucose), corn oil and corn-dried dextrins. Sulfur is also commonly employed in the manufacture of cane and beet sugar.

Artificial Colors

The addition of artificial colors (coal-tar dyes) to foods—permitted by Federal regulations—appears to be another major source of clinical reactions in highly susceptible patients otherwise avoiding major sources of chemical additives and contaminants.

To be certain that these reactions were attributable to dyes and not to other additives or to the food as such, three patients, giving this history and also highly susceptible to other chemical additives, ingested in spring water the amount of dye (Amaranth No. 2) calculated to have been present in a large serving of colored gelatin. Two of the subjects developed severe reactions when tested blindly to this material.

Artificially colored citrus fruit has also been strongly suspected in this group of patients, but this possible source of chemical contamination of fresh fruit has not been separated from the potentiality of contamination arising from the fungicide treatment of citrus crates. The additional factors of sweetening agents and canning processes must also be considered in interpreting reactions to canned citrus juices.

Several patients in this group under discussion have reported unquestionable reactions after eating dyed sweet potatoes, whereas *undyed* sweet potatoes may be used. Dyed sweet potatoes may usually be employed if carefully peeled. As a practical point, the common practice of dying sweet potatoes may usually be detected by noting the presence of dye on the broken ends of tubers. Similar reactions have been traced to the increasing practice of dying white potatoes red. A listing of other commercially colored foods will be given in the summary.

Individuals known to be highly susceptible to and avoiding other incriminated chemical exposures may react, either acutely or chronically, to artificially colored foods and drinks. The most sharp reactions have occurred to the presence of coal-tar dyes in imitation fruit drinks and in alcoholic beverages.

For instance, food diary evidence correlated the ingestion of an artificially colored grape flavored soft drink with epileptiform seizures in a 15 year old boy. Individual food ingestion tests with chemically uncontaminated grapes, commercial grapejuice and various sugars failed to react, but the trial ingestion of the suspected soft drink precipitated a typical attack. It should be mentioned, however, that this beverage also contained a chemical preservative and that the subject was aware of the identity of the test material. Avoidance of the major sources of chemically contaminated foods and other major chemical exposures relieved both his seizures and chronic fatigue. Several other patients, including the first case report of this article, have reacted acutely to the ingestion of alcoholic beverages containing coal-tar colors.

Artificial Sweeteners

Although many chemically susceptible patients have reported reactions to saccharine and Sucaryl and claim to profit by their *avoidance,* neither has as yet been subjected to controlled conditions of testing.

Foods Exposed to Gas

Most bananas are artificially ripened by exposure to ethylene gas immediately before their distribution in retail markets. The longer the interim after this exposure, the more readily bananas are tolerated by those highly susceptible to chemical exposures. This variability probably accounts for the fact that chemically susceptible patients sometimes seem to react to bananas and at other times seem able to eat them without apparent trouble. Naturally ripened bananas may sometimes be differentiated from gassed bananas by their black seeds and small speckled spots on their skins, in contrast to white seeds and large blackened areas of the skin at points where gassed bananas had been bruised in handling or shipping.

Certain other fruits are sometimes stored in the presence of ethylene and other gasses. But since the buyer usually is unaware of this possible source of contamination and since most fruits are contaminated in various other ways, this exposure has not been subjected to controlled testing.

Certain individuals of this group under consideration are also apparently susceptible to coffee. Although many are truly coffee sensitive, as determined by the ingestion of electrically roasted coffee, some are able to drink electrically roasted coffee but react to gas roasted coffee. How commonly the universal practice of roasting coffee over a gas flame contributes to the extraordinarily high incidence of apparent sensitivity to coffee has not been investigated statistically.

In 1950, the writer reported 6 cases of apparent sensitivity to cane, as determined by performing individual ingestion tests with granulated cane sugar (34). But as the chemical additive and contaminant problem later unfurled, it was subsequently learned that each of these patients was also highly susceptible to various chemical exposures. This observation initiated an investigation of the possible ways in which cane sugar might be contaminated chemically. The major source of chemical contamination is believed to occur in the *process of clarification* of the cane syrup as it is filtered through bone char. From time to time, these filters are washed, dried and reactivated at 1,000 degrees over a gas-fired flame. The char is believed to absorb the products of combustion of the gas and to impart these contaminants to subsequent filtrates.

In order to check this hypothesis, several subjects with *other* aspects of the chemical susceptibility problem and having apparent reactions to cane, failed to react when tested blindly with a special lot of cane sugar which was manufactured by means of a process by-passing bone char filtration. However, a few individuals have been observed subsequently who are apparently susceptible to cane as such, since they manifest unmistakable clinical symptoms after taking either of the above samples.

The manufacture of beet and corn sugar often involves similar processes.

Containers

The possibility that foods may be chemically contaminated by plastic wrappers and other containers is also difficult to evaluate because of the range of materials employed for this purpose and the difficulty of sorting out this possible source of contamination from others. However, there is no doubt that such chemical contamination may exist.

The writer has unmistakable evidence indicating chemical contamination of food stored in covered plastic freezer dishes, whereas the same lot of fresh food has been taken by the same person without reaction. A few extraordinarily susceptible persons have apparently reacted to foods stored in open glass containers in plastic lined refrigerators. This type of reaction is reduced or eliminated by storage of food in tightly fitted glass dishes. Unfortunately, enamel-lined refrigerators and deep freezes are no longer manufactured.

Generally speaking, the more flexible and odorous the plastic, the more it is apt to contaminate the food in which it is wrapped. Also, the longer the food remains in such a container and the more liquid or intimate the phase of contact, the more likely chemical contamination is to occur. Lee (35) pointed out that if a given wrapper may be filed without the development of an odor, it probably is not a significant factor in contaminating the food with which it is in contact. This important subject deserves a more thorough investigation in patients known to be susceptible to various other aspects of the chemical environment.

Citrus fruit is commonly packed in crates impregnated with a fungicide. Although this possible source is strongly suspected and has been incriminated as an *inhalant,* it has not been incriminated as an *ingestant* because of the difficulty of obtaining unsprayed and undyed citrus fruit packed in this manner. The odor of the presence of a peck of citrus fruit which had been packed in a diphenol impregnated case in the home of a patient with this clinical problem has been incriminated. Respiratory symptoms developed each time this person entered the portion of her home where these oranges were stored. Her husband then washed each orange in hot soapy water, brushing each fruit separately, but the odor still lingered and continued to cause acute respiratory symptoms. Somewhat later, this patient became acutely ill and was confined to her bed during the process of moving, with the complaints of asthma and headache. Her husband then recalled that her asthma had started shortly after packing cases had been brought into the home. Her symptoms subsided after the citrus packing boxes had been removed but recurred when the same boxes were brought back into the home without the subject's knowledge. This patient also becomes chronically depressed after eating commercially available oranges regularly, but is able to eat with impunity oranges known not to have been sprayed, dyed or packed in fungicide-treated cartons.

It should also be pointed out that packing cases and express cars once contaminated with DDT and similarly acting chlorinated hydrocarbon insecticides retain this contamination for long peri-ods and may subsequently contaminate other loads. This type of chemical contamination may explain the unusual case who is able to use naturally grown wheat which is transported from the producer in sealed milk cans but not the same wheat which is packaged in paper or cardboard and shipped several hundred miles by express. This type of chemical contamination under-scores the desirability of having local sources of produce which may be transferred directly from producer to consumer without the necessity of passing through the usual commercial channels.

The observation that certain patients, susceptible to other chemical additives and contaminants, reacted to foods canned in lined tins but not to the same raw or uncanned food prompted an investigation of the possible contaminating significance of can linings. This problem was difficult to study because of the fact that many fruits and vegetables were also sprayed or contaminated by other processes prior to canning. Consequently, observations were limited to salmon canned in glass as contrasted with salmon canned in tins having the usual golden-brown inner linings, and with garden fresh tomatoes of known cultural pedigree as compared with commercial tomatoes canned in lined and unlined tins. When these foods were given to selected patients, otherwise avoiding chemical additives and contaminants to which they were known to be susceptible, *acute reactions* to salmon and tomato canned in lined tins occurred.

Reactions failed to occur to the same foods canned in glass, to *fresh* salmon or tomatoes, or to tomatoes canned in *unlined* tins. Although the opportunity was not present to test identical sources of salmon and tomato prior to and following canning in metal, the group of patients under investigation have been able to eat fresh salmon or frozen fresh salmon (i.e., the intact fish) and field-ripened tomatoes without apparent trouble. This type of evidence and the continued observations of many patients suggest that the phenolic resins and related materials most com-monly entering the manufacture of can linings presumably contaminate the contents of the can. Due to the well-known volatility of phenolic compounds, it appears that such materials are also at least in part responsible for the characteristic differences in taste between such items as tinned versus untinned salmon, peaches, and certain other foods almost invariably canned in heavily lined tins.

Once this major source of food contamination by means of chemicals was recognized, the additional *avoidance* of foods canned in this manner by certain persons highly susceptible to other chemical exposures has resulted in the relief of their residual chronic symptoms.

Waxes

Certain foods waxed with a heavy coating of paraffin, such as rutabagas and parsnips, also have been shown to cause acute symptoms in certain patients highly susceptible to chemical exposures and otherwise avoiding them. Wax particles adhere to cut surfaces in the ordinary process of peeling such waxed vegetables. This may be demonstrated by immersing a previously waxed and peeled root in boiling water. Under such circumstances wax droplets rise to the top of the water as contrasted to the similar immersion of the same *unwaxed* peeled vegetable used as a control. Although these reactions are believed to be attributable to the waxing process and the adherence of wax particles to the vegetable, the opportunity of testing the same lot of vegetables prior to and following waxing has not been present.

Cucumbers, green peppers and certain fruits are commonly waxed more lightly and polished. Their ingestion has also been followed by acute *reactions* in this type of patient whereas the same vegetables of known cultural pedigree have been eaten without trouble. Although peeling a waxed cucumber apparently avoids this source of chemical contamination, peeling a green pepper is less feasible. Peeling an apple may also eliminate this source but, as previously described, it is ineffective in counteracting spray residues which apparently penetrate the entire fruit.

Glycols

Although a few patients have reported reactions to foods containing added glycols, especially certain dry cereal products and prepared cocoanut, a detailed study of this possible source of food contamination has not been made.

Antibiotics and Hormones

There are many potential sources of chemical contamination of meat, poultry and fish. These include the common practice of implanting synthetic hormones (usually stilbestrol) in the flesh of the animal and feeding antibiotics and tranquilizers. The latter seems to be an increasingly common practice in shipment immediately prior to slaughter. There is also the officially approved practice of dipping chicken and certain other fowl in antibiotic solutions, as well as the addition of coal-tar dyes and certain other chemical agents in the processing of meats.

As a result of this profusion of potential chemical contamination in the production of meat and fowl, it has only been possible to differentiate between commercially available sources of these foods, on the one hand, as against the same foods of known cultural and technological pedigree, on the other. The fact remains that many patients presenting aspects of the chemical susceptibility problem as described and otherwise avoiding incriminated sources of these contaminants react to most sources of commercially available meat and poultry. Unless a true food susceptibility exists, these same patients are able to eat the same foods known to have been grown and processed in the absence of the above mentioned techniques and in the absence of the animals having been fed forage sprayed or otherwise treated with chemical insecticide-oil mixtures for insect control.

Many of the same group of patients have observed that they are able to eat fresh fish or that frozen in *large* pieces and sawed into smaller portions while still frozen, whereas they react to the same fish which was frozen in pound lots. One wonders if this is not due to the permissible practice of dipping fish in *antibiotic solutions*—there being a much larger surface available for chemical contamination under these circumstances.

Miscellaneous

The possibility that *chemical preservatives* of foods may be major sources of reactions in persons known to be susceptible to other facets of the chemical environment is urgently in need of study. Although suggestive evidence incriminating preservatives in foods has existed in several instances—sufficient to cause patients to abstain voluntarily from such foods—multiple chemical exposures have almost always been involved.

The possible deleterious effects of foods grown on chemically fertilized soils shown to be contaminated as a result of the repeated application of potent chemical mixtures for the abatement of insects and weeds, or both, have not been investigated.

To be certain that such factors were *not* operating as additional sources of chemical contaminants, the chemically less-contaminated foods used as controls were obtained from so-called "organic" farms in which approved practices had been employed for several previous years. Although this has encouraged so-called organic plant culture for food purposes or for the feeding of animals later to be used as human food, this is not to be taken either as a blanket indictment of other practices or as a blanket endorsement of what is usually referred to as organic farming and gardening. Indeed, certain farmers who advertise their produce as *organically grown* regularly employ insecticide sprays, fumigation (sometimes required by law) and certain other practices that have been *incriminated* in the investigation of certain patients known to be highly susceptible to a wide range of chemical excitants.

Consequently, in the present unsatisfactory state of agricultural affairs—as far as the chemical environment is concerned—only those individual producers are currently recommended whose foods have consistently been tolerated by a large group of these diagnosed and controlled patients. This has usually entailed a visit to such farms and, in certain instances where a question of doubt exists as to the practices actually employed, valuable information has been obtained by interviewing a given farmer's neighbors.

The economic pressures to employ chemical practices in agriculture which insure against loss, improve the appearance, yield and keeping qualities of produce are so great that reliable producers sometimes *deviate from their former practices*. Several such instances have been uncovered. The only way in which this has been accomplished to date has been by the report of several correctly diagnosed and controlled patients suspecting a given source of supply. When such cases are investigated, the cause of the chemical contamination usually has been uncovered.

Because of these various factors increasing the costs of food production, persons demanding chemically less-contaminated foods should be prepared to pay premium prices for this type of quality.

Summary

These observations—although preliminary and far from complete—emphasize several important points:

1) Chemical contamination of a given food often occurs as a result of multiple cultural and processing techniques. The significance of any given procedure may be determined only when it has been separated from *other* potentially contaminating processes.

2) The role of any given chemical food contaminant may best be appraised by observations in patients who are known to manifest other aspects of the clinical problem of susceptibility to chemical additives and contaminants, at a time when other such exposures are avoided and the individual is symptom-free.

3) The possibility that a true susceptibility may *exist* to the chemically uncontaminated form of *any* food is always present and further complicates the detection of reactions to chemical additives and contaminants.

These points underscore the following statement: To evaluate the role of a given chemical food contaminant on health and to *differentiate these effects* from other co-existing chemical contaminants and from food allergy *per se* requires the presence of: 1) Food sources of known cultural and processing pedigree; 2) Specifically diagnosed patients in respect to their demonstrated susceptibility to chemical exposures and specific foods; and 3) A knowledge of the dynamic nature of both processes.

For instance, clearest test results are obtained in chemically susceptible patients who have been avoiding all known sources of chemical additives and contaminants of their environment for several days prior to these experimental exposures. Susceptibility to chemically uncontaminated foods is likewise best demonstrated by a test reexposure in a person who had previously been regularly exposed but who has been avoiding the food in question for a period of several days prior to such a test (13,16). In other words, testing for *chemical contaminants of food* and *foods per se* should be attempted in a *non-adapted phase* in order to demonstrate the presence of diagnostically significant acute reactions.

B. WATER ADDITIVES AND CONTAMINANTS

Chlorine

Watson and Kibler (36) were apparently the first to demonstrate the existence of susceptibility to chlorinated water. Chlorination of the water supply is such a common cause of chronic symptoms of the type described in patients susceptible to other facets of the chemical environment that it must be tested for in all instances if such exposures exist. This is best accomplished by the use of spring water during periods of comprehensive environmental control and then returning to the former chlorinated water supply. Although testing commonly has to be done with water that is both chlorinated and fluoridated, cases in which this combination has been incriminated usually have observed reactions from drinking water which had been chlorinated only.

Some, in whom the susceptibility has been of lesser degree, have been able to drink boiled chlorinated drinking water whereas unboiled drinking water was not tolerated. Presumably this is the result of the chlorine being highly volatile.

Certain persons with advanced susceptibility to the chemical environment react quickly to attempts to swim in chlorinated pools, whereas no difficulty is experienced in swimming in natural waters. A few have reacted to the inhalation of the odors of indoor chlorinated swimming pools, as previously noted.

Fluorine

The possible effects of fluoridation of drinking water has not been studied by the writer, since the water supply of this area is both chlorinated and fluoridated and non-chlorinated-fluoridated water from the same source is not readily available for test purposes. Neither has the possibility of certain other additives to the water supply been investigated.

The use of chlorinated-fluoridated water for washing foods does not ordinarily cause symptoms even in the most highly susceptible, but permitting foods to *stand* in this water prior to cooking has been incriminated in several cases. Also, inhalation of the steam of boiling chlorinated-fluoridated water in cooking or from running a hot tub in a closed bathroom or from steam radiators has been demonstrated as the cause of symptoms in certain highly susceptible persons.

Softened Water

The tendency to soften all water entering the kitchen is one of the built-in potential hazards of present-day home construction. Although this water treatment apparently may be tolerated by many, a minority may become highly susceptible to it and be made unexplainably ill by it. Whereas softened water may be used with advantage for all other purposes, *unsoftened* water should be available for *drinking and cooking*. This simply means having an extra tap in the kitchen. The positive correlation of *longevity* with hardness of the water supply is of interest in this connection (37).

C. BIOLOGICAL DRUGS

Preservatives

One of the causes of reactions to repeated doses of allergenic extracts is the existence of susceptibility to the chemical preservatives in such biological materials. This was observed independently by Glaser (38) and the writer (5).

This usually manifests with the gradual onset of bizarre reactions—either local or constitutional in type—often several months or years after the onset of injection therapy. Such reactions persist to about the same degree or increase despite repeated reductions in the potency of the active ingredients. This interpretation of reactions is established by their presence from the injection of phenol-containing diluent and their absence following the injection of phenol-free extracts containing the same dose of active principles.

Several patients known to have been highly susceptible to other facets of the chemical problem have developed constitutional symptoms following intradermal skin tests with phenol-containing extracts. The most extreme instance of this type observed was that of rapidly progressive headache, nausea, dizziness and faintness immediately following four intradermal injections to which there was no *local* reaction. Identical responses occurred each subsequent time that phenol-containing extracts were employed but not when phenol-free extracts were used, both having been injected blindly as far as the patient was concerned.

Because of the frequency of reactions to phenol in this group of patients, it has been necessary to maintain a set of phenol-free allergenic extracts for the past several years. A satisfactory preservative has not been found as yet; both Zephirin and Merthiolate not only were associated with occasional reactions but in the concentrations used, permitted mold growth. Preservative-free allergenic extracts have the obvious disadvantage of needing to be replaced frequently and requiring bacteriologic techniques in handling.

Reactions to the injection of liver extract, insulin, epinephrine and certain other biological extracts containing chemical preservatives may also be traced to the *preservatives.* But, since either the active principles, excipients (39) or preservatives may be incriminated as causes of such drug reactions, it is often exceedingly difficult to be certain that the preservative is involved. Materials, such as epinephrine for instance, are so unstable in the absence of chemical preservatives that they cannot be secured for test purposes (40).

A few patients, having other facets of the chemical problem, have been observed to develop large local reactions to troublesome general effects from each injection of liver extract, irrespective of the brand, but were able to eat liver either in daily or intermittent amounts. The questions of insulin reactions have not been investigated by the writer in this connection.

It is interesting to speculate that so-called epinephrine-fastness occurring in the continued treatment of bronchial asthma might possibly be explained on the basis of a susceptibility to and development of an addiction-type response to the chemical preservatives of the preparation. Lessening of the immediate beneficial effect of repeated injections as well as the progressive need for more frequent and larger doses suggests such a mechanism.

Dyes

Coal-tar dyes have long been used in drug manufacture. Although this subject has not been studied extensively, the writer has seen a few instances in which the dyes employed in Premarin have apparently been responsible for reactions following maintenance or intermittent dosage of this biological product in individuals highly susceptible to the ingestion of chemical dyes. At least, material supplied by the manufacturer,* known to be free of both chemical dyes and excipients (cornstarch), have been tolerated by these individuals.

Other Materials

The possibility of other sources of chemical contamination of biological drugs cannot be excluded. In addition to preservatives and dyes, these include plastic encapsulating materials, artificial sweeteners and flavors, as well as the source materials as a result of treatment with solvents and many other chemical agents. The incorporation of mineral oil and other synthetically derived materials to delay the absorption of biological extracts requires further observation to evaluate possibilities of reaction, since mineral oil is capable of inducing contact and ingestant reactions.

---

* Furnished through the courtesy of Ayerst, McKenna & Harrison.

Part V
CHEMICAL DRUGS, COSMETICS
and
PERSONAL CONTACTS
INTRODUCTION

IN VIEW OF the extensive literature dealing with reactions to chemically derived drugs, cosmetics, contact dermatitis and other contactant reactions, these subjects will be presented briefly. The main point to be emphasized here is the interrelationship existing between these reactions and susceptibility to other facets of the chemical environment existing in the same person.

This emphasis on the characteristic overlapping tendency and multiplicity of response of individuals to various chemical materials has not been brought out by concise one-track case reports or by studies showing the relative incidence of reactions to individual chemical agents. As a consequence, the *reaction-proneness* of certain persons and their tendency to develop new susceptibilities is frequently underestimated.

A. SYNTHETIC DRUGS

The tendency toward *multiple reactions* to related materials is no where observed more clearly than with reactions to chemical drugs. In fact, this tendency to react to many different drugs is so marked in certain individuals that sharp differences of opinion may arise between such patients—who are suspicious of *all* drugs —and their physicians, who tend to think of drug reactions as independent entities. Because of their proneness to drug reactions from past experiences, on the one hand, and the apparent inability of many physicians to understand this apprehension, on the other hand, many individuals afflicted in this manner have

[*85*]

become increasingly loath to seek medical care. Indeed, some patients stick tenaciously to a certain physician, not because he has helped them but because he has never made them *worse!*

Physicians need to be more alerted to this proneness to reaction to chemical drugs because of the ease with which such persons may be harmed. The tendency for individuals, already susceptible to certain facets of the chemical environment, to react to chemically derived drugs is shown by the questionnaire evidence in two series of cases. The first series of 80 chemically susceptible patients was studied by means of an early and relatively incomplete form. Approximately 50 per cent of this group were known to react to aspirin, barbiturates and sulfonamides—an extraordinarily high percentage.

The second series of 250 patients selected on the basis of known reactions to one or more facets of the chemical environment were questionnaired by means of a more complete list of drugs. Between one-quarter and one-third of this group claimed to react to aspirin, barbiturates and sulfonamides. These drugs were followed closely by antihistamines, local anesthetics and synthetic vitamins. The relatively lower incidence of reported drug reactions in the latter group is apparently the result of including a larger number of less advanced cases in this series (1958) than in the former (1952). The incidence of reactions to other drugs is shown in the accompanying table.

In general, the more advanced and long standing the illness and the more drug therapy the patient has received, the greater the number of synthetic drugs suspected of causing reactions. Moreover, individuals known to be highly susceptible to certain aspects of the chemical environment seem more prone to manifest untoward symptoms to treatment with synthetic drugs. Such reactions also tend to develop after shorter periods of therapy than occur in less susceptible persons or those in the absence of such a history.

A *synthetically derived* substance may cause a reaction in a chemically susceptible person when the same material of *natural origin* is tolerated, despite the two substances having identical *chemical* structures. This point is illustrated by the frequency of clinical reactions to synthetic vitamins—especially vitamins B_1

	1952 Series				1958 Series			
	Total Cases	80		Per Cent	Total Cases	250		Per Cent
Aspirin	38	—	47.5			77	—	34.0
Barbiturates	36	—	45.0			60	—	24.0
Sulfonamides	42	—	52.5			59	—	23.6
Antihistamines	30	—	37.5			56	—	22.4
Novocaine	13	—	18.7			56	—	22.4
Vitamins	24	—	30.0			39	—	13.6
Benzedrine	17	—	21.2			25	—	10.0
Demerol	11	—	13.7			24	—	9.6
Pentothal						17	—	6.8
Diodrast						14	—	5.6
Phenolphthalein						12	—	4.8
Privine						9	—	3.6
Stilbestrol						8	—	3.2
Amidopyrine						8	—	3.2
Butesin Picrate						6	—	2.4
Acetanilide						5	—	2.0
Pontocaine						5	—	2.0
Thorazine						4	—	1.6
Dolophine						3	—	1.2
Bromsulphthalein						2	—	0.8
Decholin						2	—	0.8
Diodoquin						2	—	0.8
Diamox						2	—	0.8
Butazolidine						2	—	0.8
Antibuse						2	—	0.8
Furadantin						1	—	0.4

and C—when these naturally occurring vitamins are tolerated. There is also other evidence indicating that the biological activity of synthetic and natural vitamins is not identical (41).

Finally, it should be emphasized that these tables showing the relative incidence of reactions to common drugs in highly susceptible patients consist only of questionnaire evidence. Because of the hazards involved, no attempt was made to confirm these reactions, although several had been confirmed as a result of accidental exposures.

B. COSMETICS AND PERFUMES

As with drugs designed for topical application, reactions in chemically susceptible persons may occur to the active chemical ingredients, their bases, artificial colors, scents, preservatives or other chemical ingredients or contaminants. In view of the number of such possibilities, involving both synthetic and natural ingredients, it is often difficult to trace reactions to tne responsible material or materials. At times, *combinations of circumstances* give rise to reactions. For instance, a clinically detectible response may occur only when a given material comes in contact with abraded skin, or to contact plus light exposure, or when combined with various other precipitating factors.

In general, however, as far as the majority of chemically susceptible persons are concerned, the scent of cosmetics is by far the most troublesome feature. Although some are much more susceptible to inhalation or contact with cosmetics and perfumes than others, those susceptible to numerous other facets of the chemical environment seem to be potentially more susceptible to cosmetics and perfumes than those without such a history. The most highly susceptible may be not only unable to wear various cosmetics and perfumes but unable to remain in the presence of others who are wearing them.

From a practical standpoint, this problem usually is handled by the avoidance of *all* perfumes, although a given person may be able to tolerate certain types or brands. Cosmetics and ointments made up entirely of natural ingredients in the absence of artificial colors, scents and preservatives are apt to be tolerated. Unfortunately, these preparations have the disadvantage of not being readily available and often requiring refrigeration.

Problems involved with the personal use of scented soaps, shampoos and various other toilet articles have been discussed earlier.

C. MISCELLANEOUS CONTACTS

The major problems not previously discussed center around reactions to textiles and their finishes, and other plastics.

Textiles and Finishes

In general, the less the odor of textiles and plastics the less their tendency to cause reactions in chemically susceptible individuals. In this connection, *rayon* and *nylon* seem to cause far less trouble in this group of patients than other woven synthetic fabrics. Many of the contactant type of reactions to synthetic textiles may be due in part—or entirely—to the *finishes* of these materials (42). Several instances have been observed by the writer in which unquestionable reactions occurred to *finished nylon products* when the same patient had been able to wear a square yard of *unfinished nylon fabric* pinned to the inner side of his pajamas without evidence of reaction. However, the fact remains that practically all *nylon* garments and hosiery are "finished," although there is considerable variability in the tolerance to these finishes among patients. Some brands may be used by certain patients while others may not.

Cotton goods also may be finished in a manner causing reactions in certain patients of this group. Although cotton materials often are less troublesome *after laundering,* some persons remain highly susceptible to certain cotton fabrics despite repeated washings. These persistent causes of reactions are most commonly attributable to the *plastic-starch treatment* of cottons, especially bed linens.

The effects of plastic-impregnated linens must be carefully differentiated from contamination of fabrics as a result of laundering, for either may induce reactions in chemically susceptible individuals. Certain of these patients have demonstrated reaction to contact with cottons which have been washed with detergents, bleached, or dried in a gas fired drier. Each of these sources of chemical exposure must also be differentiated from each other as well as from contact-type reactions attributable to the cornstarch content of sheeting, which sometimes occurs in individuals who are also highly sensitive to corn.

Aside from contact dermatitis from dyed woolens, the processing of wool does not seem to be a major factor in causing reactions in chemically susceptible persons. However, a true susceptibility to wool, both as a contactant and as an inhalant (43), is common. Wool, being more *abrasive* than certain other fabrics, may also cause extreme physical irritation of the skin.

Other Plastics

In general, the greater the *odor* and *flexibility* of a plastic the more likely it is to result in both inhalant and contactant reactions. Although contact-type reactions have been reported to a wide range of plastics, their occurrence in a given group of patients is not as high as might be expected. Occasional instances of contact reactions to prolonged direct contact with formica and vinyl table and counter tops have been noted. Bakelite, of the type formerly employed in the manufacture of telephones, has not been incriminated but the new colored plastic telephones may cause both inhalant and contact type responses.

Plastic jewelry, combs, powder cases, brushes, purses, pencils and pens may cause reactions in this group of patients but only rarely are incriminated as contactants. Prosthetic devices such as spectacle frames, hearing aids and dentures are more apt to be associated with chronic reactions because of the more constant exposures involved. The occasional person who is intolerant to acrylic dentures and plastic fillings presents a particularly difficult problem. The most satisfactory answer to this problem involving plastic spectacles and dentures is to construct these devices from metals. The question of reaction to other prosthetic devices is too specialized to be considered here.

Part VI

TREATMENT

Introduction

TREATMENT OF the manifestations of chemical susceptibility with synthetic chemical drugs usually is contra-indicated, since these materials tend to *increase the burden* to which such persons are attempting adaptation. Not only may susceptibility spread to such man-made foreign substances but the body seems to resent maintenance-dose medications aimed at limited mechanisms. As a result of these so-called anti-drug responses, physicians attempting to treat the *effects of illness* frequently find that they are also treating the effects of past and present drug therapy.

As long as chronic symptoms are perpetuated by frequent or continuous chemical exposures to which susceptibility exists, a more fundamentally sound basis of therapy is needed. In the writer's experience, the following program, designed to *reduce* rather than *increase* chemical exposures, has been most helpful.

1) Chemical and other environmental excitants capable of inducing susceptibility and perpetuating chronic syndromes are suspected on the basis of probability and details of the history.

2) Suspected exposures are eliminated *concurrently*. This tends to induce non-adapted responses in which later re-exposures are apt to precipitate acute immediate reactions of diagnostic significance.

3) Materials so incriminated are then eliminated, if possible. Although such a program is detailed and restrictive, it remains the most workable long-term approach to the clinical problem presented by a chemically susceptible person.

4) Certain additional therapeutic measures in accordance with the apparent acid-hypoxia-endocrine-enzymatic mechanism of

[*91*]

these responses (44,45,46,47) are also helpful.

Descriptive differences between chronic effects from maintenance doses and acute symptoms following isolated exposures to the same material suggests the operation of somewhat different mechanisms. Although the identity of these processes is not known, empirically, they seem to respond to different types of treatment.

A. THERAPY OF ACUTE REACTIONS

The basic principles in the treatment of acute reactions center about therapy aimed both at apparent mechanisms and the rapid elimination of excitants. These measures are most effective if instituted immediately and carried out conjointly.

Ingested Chemicals

Acute reactions resulting from the ingestion of chemical additives and contaminants of foods, biological drugs and water supplies, or chemical drugs are treated by emptying the gastrointestinal tract as soon as possible. Although this sometimes occurs as a result of the excitant itself, one is not justified in waiting for such a spontaneous effect. It may not occur; it may be considerably delayed, or the total effect on motility of the gastrointestinal tract may be characterized by constipation.

Although the alimentary canal may be emptied by means of various laxatives and enemas, the writer prefers the oral administration of the bicarbonates of sodium and potassium because of their *multiple effects*. This mixture not only exerts a laxative action but also combats the apparent acidity involved (44,45) and, if employed in the correct proportions for given individuals, seems to have a diuretic effect. Finally, it may also exert a mode of action apparently not dissimilar to that of ACTH and related materials (47).

Alkali salts are administered as soon as possible after cause and effect relationships of acute reactions have been demonstrated. This is accomplished by giving between 10 and 15 grams of mixed alkali (usually 2/3 sodium bicarbonate and 1/3 potassium bicarbonate) in approximately a quart of *spring water*. The use of spring water is stipulated because the dose of chemical contaminants in the amount of tap water required may induce an acute reaction, especially if generally available water supplies had been avoided. In the event a laxative effect has not occurred within two hours, an additional 5-7 grams of mixed alkali salts similarly diluted, or a spring water enema, is given.

There are certain individual differences apparently involved which, for optimum effects, may require variations in the proportions of sodium and potassium bicarbonate: the occurrence of fluid retention, as manifested by puffy eyes or other evidence of edema, or, if one is interested in a more prompt laxative action, increasing the proportion of potassium bicarbonate up to 50 per cent may be helpful. Occasionally, where it has been necessary to treat successive acute reactions in this manner, it is desirable to use magnesium oxide in the form of milk of magnesia either supplementally or intermittently for its laxative action.

In instances of severe nausea and vomiting, the alkali combination may be administered by enema, or sodium bicarbonate may be given intravenously (45). The recommended dosage is 7.5 to 10.75 grams (two to three 50.0 cc. ampules) of a 7.5 per cent solution.* This may be introduced either by an intravenous drip or by means of a 50 cc. syringe. There seems to be no contraindication to injecting the material as rapidly as may be delivered by a 21 gauge needle. Leaving the delivery needle in situ and filling the syringe by means of a larger needle facilitates the administration.

The injection is continued until acute symptoms subside; until the onset of an excessive thirst, or until the full amount has been given. If such a dose is ineffective in the treatment of an acute reaction, larger amounts usually are not helpful. Immediately prior to the onset of an excessive thirst, the patient may notice gastrointestinal rumbling or tingling of the lips or face. Occasionally, transient chilling may occur either during or immediately following an injection.

Either oral or intravenous alkali therapy—especially the latter —is contraindicated in instances of *cardiac* or *renal failure and during pregnancy*. The general safety of sodium bicarbonate intravenously has been attested by detailed observations (48).

---

* Manufactured by Abbott Laboratories, North Chicago, Illinois.

Other Acute Reactions

Acute reactions from *inhaled, injected,* or *contacted chemicals* may also be treated effectively with similar doses of alkali salts. It should be emphasized that this therapy is effective in the absence of diarrhea, although the laxative action may be additionally effective in aiding the elimination of retained fluids. As in the therapy of acute reactions resulting from ingestants, the earlier alkali treatment is started, the better.

Oxygen

Inhalation of oxygen by metal nasal catheter and Tygon tubing is effective early in the course of acute reactions from inhaled chemical exposures. The use of this special *non-odorous plastic tubing* and avoidance of *odorous rubber tubing,* masks, breathing bags and plastic tents is advisable in view of the tendency of odorous rubber and plastic to induce or perpetuate symptoms. Although oxygen may also be helpful in the therapy of acute reactions from ingested chemicals, it does not ordinarily substitute for alkali treatment.

Patients with high degrees of susceptibility to chemical exposures profit by having a small tank of oxygen in their homes for emergency use. Some find that carrying an emergency oxygen case is useful in traveling.

Drugs

A limited number of biological drugs are helpful in the treatment of acute reactions. These include such natural sympatheticomimetic preparations as ephedrine and epinephrine. *Natural* antibiotics are preferable to synthetic ones. Codeine and other opiates are preferred over synthetic analgesics. Antihistaminics, barbiturates, and other synthetically derived drugs may be helpful when used occasionally, but are preferably *avoided.*

Specific susceptibility to biologic drugs or their chemical additives and contaminants may occur, as previously described. When drug therapy is mandatory, there are times when a synthetically derived drug may be less objectionable than a biologic product to which a given individual is sensitive. But when acute reactions are adequately treated with alkalis and/or oxygen, additional drug therapy—including that with steroids—is usually not necessary.

B. THERAPY OF CHRONIC REACTIONS

Avoidance of Incriminated Offenders

The *avoidance* of incriminated excitants to which a person has been found susceptible remains the *treatment* of choice. Specific details of how this is accomplished has been touched upon earlier and will be summarized later. Although such a regimen may be highly restrictive, no equally satisfactory program is available. It is also admitted that such avoidance programs often entail considerable expense and inconvenience, especially if indoor air pollutants and chemical additives and contaminants of the food and water supplies are involved. However, if one is sufficiently sick and disabled and especially if other means of control have been exhausted—as so often is the case—such an avoidance program is readily accepted. Furthermore, the demonstration of the *causes* of illness comes as a welcome relief to many chronically sick persons.

Alkalis and Oxygen

Alkali therapy is not recommended for the treatment of chronic reactions of the type previously described and resulting from susceptibility to and exposure to chemical and other excitants. Although a maintenance dose of sodium and potassium bicarbonate may assist in the treatment of relatively minor chronic symptoms, it is usually insufficient to relieve major symptom syndromes and sometimes actually accentuates them. The writer has had the unfortunate experience of inducing sharp accentuations of status asthmaticus, protracted migraine headaches, chronic depressions, and certain other advanced *chronic* manifestations following intravenous alkali therapy.

On the other hand, certain specifically diagnosed patients may find that restrictions do not need to be quite as exacting when taking a maintenance dose of alkali salts. For instance, a correctly diagnosed patient, aged eighty-three, subject to chronic arthritis, headaches and depression when eating regularly of specific foods and especially chemical additives and contaminants of food and water, remains relatively symptom-free when avoiding exposures to which susceptibility has been demonstrated. Nevertheless, she claims to *feel better* when taking a daily dose of five grams of mixed alkali salts each morning—a program she has continued for the past decade. Each of several times that her electrolytes have been checked, normal values have been found. Although alkali therapy may be used effectively as an adjunct to an *avoidance program*, this usually is not necessary.

Oxygen therapy is of only limited value in treating chronic reactions but, as with alkali therapy, is very helpful in tiding over acute exacerbations of chronic syndromes. Again, the quicker either is instituted, the more effective.

Drugs

Patients already susceptible to certain facets of the chemical environment are known for their ability to develop *new* susceptibilities to *other* chemical and biologic exposures to which they are frequently subjected. Maintenance doses of drugs are particularly effective in inducing such chronic syndromes. Since maintenance *drug dosage* tends to add to the patient's load of materials to which he is attempting adaptation, they are generally contraindicated. A spread of susceptibility to such chemically derived drugs is to be expected. Not infrequently patients give the history of having had to discard one such preparation after another.

Steroids are not recommended in the treatment of chronic reactions, although ACTH seems to be less troublesome than the others. They may be temporarily effective; however, such programs are not only expensive but frequently result in troublesome complications. One of the most troublesome features of steroid therapy is the tendency for symptoms to be accentuated immediately after these drugs are stopped (49). But even more important, the patient previously treated with steroids seems to be much more difficult to diagnose and treat specifically thereafter. Although the complications of prolonged steroid therapy may be less troublesome than at first suspected, these preparations do *not* provide satisfactory answers to long-term chronic illness.

Specific Injection Therapy

Certain chemically susceptible patients, also sensitive to house dust, have obtained considerable relief of chronic symptoms as a result of receiving regular injections of *house dust extract,* although preservative-free materials may be required. A similar mutual relationship between chemical susceptibility and pollen, mold, and food sensitivity has also been observed. Despite the helpfulness of such a specifically oriented injection schedule, it does not ordinarily provide completely satisfactory relief of symptoms. Unfortunately, it has the additional disadvantage of adding to the load of materials to which a chronically sick person is attempting adaptation. This interpretation apparently accounts for the necessity of *discontinuing all injection therapy* in certain instances.

It should be emphasized, however, that certain individuals with multiple susceptibilities do not require injection therapy with extracts of house dust, pollens, or spores *when avoiding* chemical and food exposures to which susceptibility has been demonstrated.

Two unusually interesting patients, both of whom are susceptible to house dust and chemical excitants, obtain a period of relief of their chronic symptoms only as a result of house dust injections *containing phenol* as a preservative. This has been demonstrated repeatedly by employing phenol-containing and phenol-free extracts blindly. Both persons identified the beneficial effects produced by the preservative containing injections as against a nil effect of the same dose of phenol-free house dust extract. The possibility of this being an adapted response to the phenol cannot be excluded, but injections of the phenol-containing diluent only were less effective than when combined with the usual dose of house dust.

General Measures

Control of infectious processes, especially amoebiasis and other chronic parasitic and microbial infections is helpful, since invading microorganisms and inanimate excitants apparently impinge on common defenses—including the ability to develop immunologically protective responses. Similarly, the control of thyroid and other endocrine deficiencies should not be neglected.

A program of regular active physical exercise or other measures to increase and maintain muscular tone and circulation are sufficiently beneficial to be all that may be required to counteract low grade chronic reactions.

Avoidance of *excessive* physical fatigue may also be of assistance but, more commonly, fatigue, irritability, and the tendency for inter-personal and emotional responses are more readily demonstrable as *effects* rather than additional *causes* of illness in the persons studied (17,18).

C. PROPHYLAXIS

Specifically Diagnosed Cases

As previously stated, the patient already susceptible to certain excitants tends to develop a *spread* of the process to other facets of the chemical environment to which chronic exposures are maintained. Conversely, when diagnosed patients *avoid* as many chemical exposures as possible, the process is far less apt to spread. Furthermore, such a program usually is associated with a decreasing degree of susceptibility to incriminated chemical excitants. This course of events was illustrated in the second case report, in which chemical exposures that formerly induced *acute* depressions subsequently precipitated only episodes of rhinitis and coughing.

But once a high degree of susceptibility to a chemical excitant has developed, even though it may be *reduced as a result of avoidance* it may be reactivated quickly by later chronic exposures. Intermittent exposures may do likewise.

Specifically Undiagnosed Cases

Although the *scope* of the chemical environment precludes its avoidance prophylactically, there are specific exposures about which we, as a race, have been extraordinarily careless. Among these chronic exposures are *indoor* chemical air pollutants arising from gas utilities and other indoor hydrocarbons. Equally troublesome is the indiscriminate practice of spraying foodstuffs with insecticide-solvent mixtures. The potential dangers of these daily chemical exposures—insofar as the general health of all is concerned—is such as to warrant a far greater degree of protection, prophylactically, than presently exists.

The magnitude of the clinical problem associated with indoor hydrocarbon exposures and outdoor traffic exhausts underscores the urgent need of improvements in the design and combustion efficiency of gas kitchen ranges, heating systems and automobiles.

The downhill clinical course of many patients is also associated with the indiscriminate use of chemical drugs. Both the general public and the medical profession need to be alerted to the potentially hazardous effect of overzealous drug therapy. It is well to recall that a physician's *first responsibility* to his patient is *to do no harm*. This responsibility is rapidly becoming more hazardous, in view of the *increasing susceptibility of patients* to chemical excitants, on the one hand, and to the progressive monopolization of medical supplies by *chemically derived drugs* on the other. Indeed, this hazard is so great—insofar as certain patients are concerned—that there is no satisfactory alternative to that of determining what parts of the chemical environment may already be involved and helping the patient to *avoid* those exposures.

Part VII

CASE REPORTS

EARLIER CASE reports were selected to illustrate the development and scope of the clinical problem presented by the *chemically susceptible patient*. The following reports illustrate the applicability of the program of comprehensive environmental control and subsequent re-exposures as diagnostico-therapeutic measures.

S. D., a surgeon, 42 years old, was seen because of a progressive agitation-depression syndrome that had failed to respond satisfactorily to psychiatric management.

Following eczema in infancy, he had continued to have a dry, easily irritated skin. Acute rheumatic fever was diagnosed at twelve years, because of the occurrence of fever, painful joints, fatigue and irritability. This was treated with large doses of acetylsalicylic acid until the onset, after a few weeks, of generalized urticaria and bronchial asthma. Both manifestations subsided after this analgesic was discontinued. The rare occurrence of hives in recent years—usually occurring after eating seafood—has been treated by means of antihistaminic drugs. During the year prior to his initial visit in 1959 he had been subject to increasingly severe generalized edema. Asthma never recurred.

In 1949 he was diagnosed on x-ray evidence as having a peptic ulcer, which healed satisfactorily on medical management. His only gastrointestinal manifestations in recent years have been vomiting and/or diarrhea following seafood.

Phenergan was first taken in intermittent doses for the relief of acute rhinitis, but more recently has been used in nightly subcutaneous doses of 25-50 mgm.

Headaches, which had been present for a decade and increasingly constant for the past year, were known to have been accentuated by exposure to traffic exhausts, the odor of solvents, fresh paint, and certain other volatile hydrocarbons. Largely because of the headaches resulting from traffic odors, he moved from a metropolitan area to a small town in 1953.

Chronic fatigue had also been a major complaint since age 20. The degree of tiredness was unrelated to the amount of work done or rest obtained. Although it was worse certain days, for no apparent reason, chronic fatigue was present to some extent *every day* and came to be associated with an increasing level of generalized muscle fatigue and aching.

Becoming extremely hyperactive after using opiates, he often used meperidine for the relief of headaches. Daily injections for the control of pain had also been received during three traumatic episodes in the year prior to his first visit. He gradually drifted into taking daily injections, regularly, of Phenergan and Demerol; otherwise, he remained extremely nervous and jittery. Isolated injections of local anesthetics also increased his nervousness.

Insomnia became increasingly troublesome. Chronic fatigue, profuse perspiration, nervousness, irritability, and a progressively troublesome tremor materially interfered with his work. Sexual maladjustment and other abnormalities of behavior developed, with a progressive tendency for hyperactivity and agitation to alternate with gradually increasing episodes of fatigue, headache and depression.

This patient was hospitalized for specific diagnosis and treatment at a time when the history of apparent addiction to meperidine was not known. On the second day of fasting and the avoidance of all drugs, tobacco and other exposures previously described, he became increasingly restless, nervous, depressed and achy. All symptoms were accentuated on the third day when he developed a temperature to 102.5 degrees F. Residual myalgia, fatigue and rhinitis tapered off the fourth day.

At this point, when relatively symptom-free, he threw a window wide open—against strict orders—and air heavily polluted by refinery odors was carried in by a southeast drift wind. Soon, he began to complain of feeling flighty, jittery and tense; claimed to be unable to read comprehendingly, and seemed to be preoccupied with one-track thoughts. Insomnia and restlessness, characteristic of the early part of this attack, were followed by residual fatigue and nasal stuffiness.

After recovering from this reaction and on the seventh day of the fasting program, single foods of known cultural pedigree were returned to his diet. After several foods had been taken without incident, he reacted to potatoes boiled in spring water. His resting pulse prior to this feeding was 72; his pulse rates at 20 minute intervals following were 84, 96, and 72. Distension and gaseous eructations occurred immediately. A severe headache developed at two hours and was followed shortly by vomiting. Restlessness and insomnia characterized the first few hours of this reaction; depression persisted through the night. Despite emptying the gastrointestinal tract by means of alkali salts and milk of magnesia, a weight gain of two pounds was noted the following morning. He then gave the additional history of commonly vomiting after "eating out," at which time he usually ate a *baked potato*.

Although natural (chemically uncontaminated) corn failed to react, commercially available *corn meal* and *corn sugar* were followed by immediate abdominal distress and gaseousness. Projectile vomiting occurred two hours later. He remained awake throughout the night, becoming extremely depressed toward morning, at which time he threatened to leave the hospital.

The first time commercially available eggs were tried, tachycardia (72:78, 94 and 78), insomnia and irritability were the only developments. He was subsequently fed eggs of known cultural pedigree, from the same source as those tolerated by other chemically susceptible patients. Increased salivation occurred immediately. A headache developed at two hours; vomiting followed. Despite a profuse diarrhea after taking alkali salts and milk of magnesia, his headache persisted and became associated with nervousness, apprehension, wringing of hands and a subsequent depression. He finally fell asleep at 4 a.m. Upon awakening at 6 a.m., he was symptom-free.

After not having reacted to *other foods* used regularly in his diet, he was checked for susceptibility to chemical contamination of the diet by means of several meals of previously *unsuspected uncommon foods* known for their chemical contamination. Nothing was observed after a breakfast of commercially available canned blueberries sweetened with Sucaryl, nor a lunch of canned tuna, canned dietetic cherries, frozen cauliflower and raw apple. Two hours after a dinner of canned salmon, canned dietetic peaches, frozen broccoli and raw celery, he noticed the recurrence of nervousness, tremor, jitteriness and hyperactivity. Insomnia persisted until 4 a.m., at which time he finally fell asleep, the phase of hyperactivity being followed by depression. Since natural—chemically uncontaminated—sources of these foods have since been tolerated, this response may be interpreted as the *cumulative effect of chemical additives and contaminants* of these foods.

At a time when symptom-free, he was discharged home on a test-compatible diet, spring water, and without drugs. During the first two days there was no immediate effect when he remained in his electrically equipped home in the summertime. He also returned to drinking local well water without reaction. However, each time his wife wore *hair spray* a typical recurrence of insomnia developed. Upon two different occasions, exposure to *fresh paint odors* at the hospital was followed by a recurrence of tremor, hyperactivity, irritability, a delayed depression, ankle edema, and a weight gain of nine pounds. Several lesser grade exposures followed breaks in the diet before a consistent chemically uncontaminated source of foods was worked out. Eggs and potato still caused severe reactions, even though *not* chemically contaminated.

He has remained symptom-free and without drugs for the past several months while following a chemically uncontaminated diet, avoiding eggs and potato. His weight now remains constant instead of fluctuating widely. He is able to work long hours without tremor and with far less fatigue than formerly, although prolonged exposure to certain anesthetic odors in the operating room are slightly troublesome. Profuse perspiration—formerly a major handicap when operating—is no longer present. Sexual adjustment is now satisfactory. He is apparently a happier and more pleasant person, insofar as his family and associates are concerned, and he is *far more productive* in his work.

Since this patient did not have a major susceptibility to *home installations* the reaction of two *other* patients upon returning home will be cited briefly to illustrate these factors.

M. W., a 42 year old housewife, subject to rhinitis since infancy and, more recently, chronic fatigue, headache and intermittent periods of depression, became symptom-free in the hospital. She was discharged on a compatible diet and water supply and without drugs.

There was no obvious reaction during the first 36 hours at home, during which time the gas kitchen stove was used only minimally. The afternoon of the second day home she used the gas kitchen stove in baking for a period of three hours. Within the first hour she had a recurrence of nasal stuffiness, followed by profuse rhinorrhea. She then became increasingly irritable and subsequently depressed. When the gas range was moved to the garage, she felt generally better. Symptoms recurred when it was *returned* to the house and used, irrespective of the type of food cooked.

Since the permanent removal of the gas range and the continued avoidance of major contaminated foods, she has remained relatively symptom-free except for occasional accidental exposures. These usually have followed visits in *other homes* or attempts to eat in poorly ventilated restaurants in which gas kitchen ranges were used.

N. R., housewife, age 31, was first seen because of repeated bouts of rhinitis, fatigue, headache, myalgia, and low-grade temperature elevations suggestive of influenza. She also complained of being dopey, groggy, unable to read comprehendingly or to think clearly. When these symptoms were intensified, she usually was depressed. At other times she was irritable, unsteady on her feet, and frequently dropped things.

She was found highly sensitive to several common foods. Although she profited by their avoidance, she remained chronically sick. The fact that she was better during summer months and on vacations when away from home; also the fact that her symptoms *recurred soon after she returned home* suggested susceptibility to house dust or indoor chemical air pollution. Although she was found skin-test-sensitive to house dust and knew that dust exposure accentuated her rhinitis, treatment at various levels with house dust extract did not afford satisfactory relief.

Her chronic symptoms during winter months were at least 50 per cent improved following the *simultaneous elimination* of her gas range, gas refrigerator and gas water heater from her kitchen and the *substitution of electrical equipment*.

Feeling relatively better most of the time after this change, she then was able to detect the effects of *other* previously unsuspected chemical exposures. One by one, acute reactions were traced to her husband's use of after-shaving lotion, spray deodorants in the bathroom, the inhalation of the odors of synthetic alcohol and synthetic vitamin preparations, the use of weed-killing sprays on the lawn, the odors of the municipal mosquito abatement spraying, odors from tarring of roofs and roads, wearing an Orlon sweater, traffic exhausts, and many others.

But despite following a restricted diet—including a chemically less contaminated food intake—she still remained inexplicably ill most of the winter months. When alternating depression and irritability-nervousness, dizziness and panic recurred in the fall of 1955, the family decided to follow through with the previous recommendation to replace their warm air furnace with hot water central heating, installing the furnace in the garage.

With the control of indoor air pollution, the avoidance of major chemically contaminated foods, and a few other specific susceptibilities, this patient has remained well. From time to time, additional chemical exposures have been detected—one of which was the odor of a colored plastic telephone. With the mother's improved health, an important and unexpected development has occurred—the better health and behavior of the grade school children in this family; they are happier, less quarrelsome, and have greatly improved in their school work.

Part VIII

INSTRUCTIONS FOR AVOIDING CHEMICAL ADDITIVES, CONTAMINANTS AND DRUGS

THE FOLLOWING brochure, to which local sources of chemically less contaminated foods may be appended, has been found helpful in the instruction of patients. However, it is *not* to be used for this purpose until *after* a patient has *answered his questionnaire,* as given in Part II.

Clinical susceptibility to gas, oil and coal—including their combustion products and related derivatives—is a common unsuspected cause of chronic illness.

The exposures to be described have been demonstrated as causative factors in the investigation of over a thousand patients susceptible to chemical additives and contaminants of air, food, water and biological drugs, as well as synthetic chemical drugs and related materials. Although no one is susceptible to *all* of these materials, a large portion of this chemical environment may be involved either by inhalation, ingestion, injection, or by contact. Once started, this process tends to increase in degree and to spread to related substances to which one is chronically exposed.

There are various stages of susceptibility to chemically contaminated air, food, water and biological drugs, synthetic drugs, cosmetics, textiles, rubber, plastics, and other chemically derived materials. When a slightly susceptible person is first adapting to oft-repeated or constant doses of one or more of these agents, he tends to remain energetic and relatively symptom-free. He may even express a liking or fondness for exposures acting in this manner.

But as adaptation to these everyday materials decreases, charac-

[*106*]

teristic overlapping and cumulative effects develop so insidiously that victims rarely know their causes. When such a person is asked about a given substance, he might reply that he liked it; that it had no apparent effect; that he disliked it, or that it made him sick. His answer would depend upon his degree of susceptibility to it and to variations in the frequency and size of exposure. For instance, a person susceptible to various chemical exposures is more apt to suspect fresh paint odors (encountered only occasionally and in relatively concentrated amounts) than the odors arising from a gas kitchen range or warm air heating system (from which he is rarely separated for more than a few hours at a time).

Whether certain chemical exposures are suspected also depends on a person's sense of smell. Although many victims of this illness have an extremely *acute* ability to detect the odors of escaping gas and other chemical fumes—far beyond that of those non-afflicted—the reverse may also be true. Certain advanced cases having an impaired sense of smell are at an additional disadvantage in protecting themselves from exposure to various chemical odors and fumes.

Individuals affected adversely by chemical additives, contaminants and drugs are apt to be sensitive to pollens, spores, animal danders, dust, or other biological materials which may cause identical symptoms. *Avoiding as many offenders as possible is indicated.*

INDOOR CHEMICAL AIR POLLUTION

Indoor chemical air pollution is primary; it must be brought under some degree of control before attempting to observe the clinical effects of *other* chemical exposures.

Homes. Indoor chemical air pollution is especially difficult to detect because of the constancy of major contributing exposures, namely, the odors and fumes from gas kitchen ranges; gas or fuel-oil space heaters; gas refrigerators and other gas burning utilities; warm air furnaces, and odors of rubber, plastic, insecticides, perfumes, detergents, bleaches and cleansers. Although susceptibility to indoor chemical air contaminants characteristically produces winter illness, it may cause perennial or summer-accentuated symptoms. With open windows, relatively more volatile summer traffic odors, which are also produced by relatively more traffic than in winter, enter homes more readily. In the presence of closed windows, evaporation of filter oils in air conditioning equipment or the odors of electric fans or other motors may be troublesome. Fans—as integral parts of warm air, hot water or electric room-heating units—are not reccommended.

Since susceptibility to chemicals usually accompanies clinical susceptibility to biological excitants, the simultaneous avoidance of *all* common exposures on the basis of probability is most apt to relieve a patient's chronic symptoms. This is best accomplished by fasting a patient in hospital quarters relatively freed of odors and fumes as well as pollens, spores, danders and dusts. During this time the patient should avoid drugs, cosmetics, tobacco and synthetic textiles in wearing apparel, and should drink only spring water. The effects of returning single chemically uncontaminated common foods is first noted. Then the effect of returning chemically contaminated foodstuffs is observed. Incriminated materials are avoided as detected.

Then the symptom-free patient on a compatible intake of food and water is returned to his previously avoided home surroundings, working conditions, local water supplies and avocations. If a person worsens after returning home under these circumstances, susceptibility to indoor air pollutants is probable. The gas kitchen range or gas or fuel-oil space heaters are first to be suspected. The effect of removing these from the home, temporarily, and returning them is noted. It should be emphasized that merely turning off the gas line to the house does *not* constitute an adequate test, since seepage from unused gas utilities may perpetuate chronic symptoms. If incriminated, it is usually necessary to replace all gas utilities with electric equipment and it may be advisable to remove all gas pipes from the house.

Warm air furnaces are also common causes of winter symptoms but this usually is best checked after the above exposures have been appraised. Warm air furnaces sometimes leak between their combustion and warm air chambers or puff when turned on, emitting combustion products through cold air intakes, floors, walls, and up stairwells and laundry chutes. Many chemically susceptible patients seem to react to the first blast of warm air when such furnaces turn on automatically.

The type of furnace fuel which is used is relatively unimportant as each has disadvantages. Gas tends to leak at various joints in the line. Oil burning furnaces have a characteristic odor which is accentuated if the storage tank is located in the basement or if it has overflowed. Coal usually is soaked with kerosene when delivered; this slowly evaporates and fouls the air of the basement. Coal-fired furnaces sometimes burn into the spiral of the stoker, smoking the basement. Fireplaces burning coal are apt to puff; those burning pine wood may also emit troublesome odors. Downdrafts in an unused fireplace flue of a double chimney may carry fumes from an adajcent flue into living quarters.

Since there are major objections to both warm air furnaces and to fuels stored or burned in the house, *electric heating* or *hot water* or *steam central heating, with the furnace located in an adjacent garage or out-building,* is recommended. Neither the furnace room nor the garage should be located in the basement. Neither should either be entered directly from the house by means of an intercommunicating passage, in view of the ease with which odors and fumes may contaminate the living quarters.

Apartment dwellers should not live adjacent to or directly above the furnace room or garage, but even upper floors may be contaminated as a result of motor exhausts of basement garages entering elevator shafts. In general, those highly susceptible to chemical additives and contaminants are more comfortable living in *all-electric* apartment buildings rather than those containing both gas and electric utilities.

Toxic insecticides, such as dieldrin, chlordane and pentachlorophenol are often used by professional exterminators for control of termites and ants. Do not permit the use of these chemicals under your home or in your attic. Arsenic is much less toxic, when control is imperative. Rugs and blankets are often mothproofed by the use of DDT and other insecticides in cleaning or in storage. Be careful to avoid such treatment.

The air of living quarters may also be fouled by the odors of sponge rubber pillows, rubber mattresses, foam upholstery, rubber rug pads, rubber or plastic backing of rugs and carpets or plastic upholstery, plastic folding doors, plastic telephones, plastic shoe bags and plastic bedding covers. Similarly, the use of perfume, cologne, scented soap and shampoo, nail polish, nail polish remover, cigarette lighters, lighter and cleaning fluids, household deodorants, disinfectants, Lysol, phenol, insecticide sprays, bleaches, cleansers containing bleach, and ammonia may not be tolerated. Many react to the odors of moth balls or crystals; floor wax; furniture, shoe or metal polishes; fresh newspapers; tobacco smoke; Christmas trees and other indoor evergreen decorations; pine oil and pine-scented cleansers and toilet articles. The majority are highly susceptible to the fumes of turpentine, mineral spirits, synthetic alcohol and evaporating paints, varnishes, shellacs, lacquers, and various solvent and/or tar-containing adhesives. *Interior decorating and the laying of tile or flooring should be done in the patient's absence and be odorless before his return.* In general, *casein* or *alkyd based paints* are better tolerated than rubber based paints or those containing turpentine or mineral spirits.

Aerosol bombs or sprays containing lindane, methoxychlor, DDT, chlordane, malathione or thiocyanates should *never* be used indoors and only with great caution outdoors. For mosquitoes, moths, flies and other insect pests, "Aerosect" aerosol bomb (Pennsylvania Engineering Co., Philadelphia 23, Pa.), containing pyrethrum and rotenone in a base of sesame oil may be used with caution. "Ortho-extrax" spray with rotenone and pyrethrum, when mixed with water, is the least harmful spray for ant invasions. However, these contain petroleum oils and should be avoided indoors.

Leaking refrigerant gas may also cause acute or chronic symptoms. This is not only used in electric refrigerators, deep freezes and air conditioning equipment, but also is the compressed repellant in most dispensers of the bomb type for insecticides, perfumes, hair sprays, whipped topping and various other foods and drugs. Leaking refrigerant is suggested by a gradually decreasing refrigerator frosted coil surface, too constant operation of the machine, or by *reactions* to stored or frozen food when the same lot of food had been tolerated *prior to* storage or freezing.

Public Places. Many patients react to the contaminated air of bus or train depots or from riding in diesel buses or trucks. Some are troubled by contact with or the odors of pine-paneled interiors; mineral oil treatment of bedding, furniture or rugs to allay dust; deodorants used in theatres, public toilets or other public places; the odors of perfume and other highly scented cosmetics emanating from crowds; perfume counters of drug and specialty stores; rubber or plastic odors of new automobiles or chlorine odors from indoor swimming pools. Some students and teachers are made mentally sluggish by inhalation of the exhausts of gas stoves in the school's cafeteria, home economics rooms, or by odors arising from improper heating or air conditioning equipment. Some persons—when otherwise avoiding major exposures —may react sufficiently to the odors of gas ranges, other unvented gas utilities and warm air heating systems to preclude shopping or visiting in quarters so equipped.

OUTDOOR AIR POLLUTION

Metropolitan outdoor air contamination is most marked downtown and in industrial areas, being heaviest in the vicinities of refineries, gas works, paint and chemical factories, rubber and sulfur processing plants, steel mills, fertilizer plants, et cetera. Those susceptible to chemical odors and fumes should try to live to the *windward side* of such metropolitan and industrial areas —as far away from them as possible. Since contamination extends peripherally along roads and railroads, such persons profit by living at least three blocks from expressways and railroads and avoiding areas of decelerating traffic, such as at bus stops and stop lights. Driving to the *windward side* of multi-laned traffic is helpful. Try to keep at least four car lengths behind other vehicles when stopping for lights or crossings. Avoid heavily traveled routes. Close your car windows and turn on inside air *only* when passing diesel trucks or buses, or when driving through excessively contaminated areas.

Ordinarily, one is less exposed to the fumes of his own vehicle when riding in the front seat and keeping rear and rear-side windows closed. Automobiles having defective exhaust or brake systems, improper carburetor adjustment, or using an excessive amount of oil, should be *repaired* or *discarded*.

Air pollution in metropolitan areas is accentuated at street level; in the basements of downtown streets; in subways; on quiet, humid or rainy days, or when the wind is blowing gently from the vicinity of refinery or industrial areas. *Visibility* is the best single *index* of *air pollution* in Chicago. Eye irritation may occur.

Air pollution is dispersed through residential areas in various ways—from traffic exhausts, home heating units, home incinerators, and spraying for insect control. Odors and fumes from burning of home refuse are highly irritating, due in part to the bulk of waxed food cartons in such dry garbage. Mosquito abatement programs or spraying lawns, gardens, orchards, farms or forests for the control of insects or weeds menaces the health of many highly susceptible persons. Such victims should request advance notification of such spraying by their neighbors or municipalities so as to be able to protect themselves or to flee from the area. Chemical air contamination, no longer limited to cities, is becoming a major problem in rural regions due to widespread spraying processes and the use of mechanized farm equipment.

Although pollens, spores and larger dust particles ordinarily are removed by the filters in air conditioning equipment, *chemical air contaminants are not removed*. In fact, chemical odors and fumes may be accentuated by evaporation of the filter oils in such equipment. Chemical fumes and cooking and smoking odors may be effectively removed only by *activated carbon filters,* provided such equipment contains a *sufficient quantity* of activated carbon for this purpose. However, such installations in warm air furnaces have not proved satisfactory. As an emergency measure, breathing through a gas mask cannister protects one from unexpected exposures such as might be encountered in driving over freshly tarred roads, through refinery areas, in the vicinity of spraying rigs or diesel trucks or buses. An activated carbon civilian defense gas mask may be purchased from surplus military supply stores. Only the cannister is to be used, as the rubber of the mask may induce additional symptoms because of its odor.

DRUGS, COSMETICS AND PERSONAL CONTACTS

Drugs. Certain biological drugs, especially those designed for injection—such as epinephrine, insulin, liver extract, allergen extracts, et cetera—usually contain phenol, chlorbutanol or other chemical preservatives capable of causing reactions in individuals highly susceptible to chemical additives.

Persons susceptible to chemicals and related materials should also avoid the use of such synthetic chemical drugs as aspirin (Anacin, Bufferin, Empirin, Empirin Compound, acetylsalicylic acid and certain cold remedies); sulfonamides; sulfur-containing preparations, barbiturates and most other sedatives; tranquilizers; antihistaminic drugs and many antibiotics. Mineral oil, petroleum jelly, vaseline or ointment bases of synthetic origin as well as preparations containing synthetic dyes, scents or preservatives may also cause trouble in these individuals. This usually means the avoidance of hand lotions, laxatives, most ointments and creams, tar and creosote-containing preparations and synthetic vitamins. The odor of or contact with synthetic alcohol and certain adhesive tapes may be troublesome. In general, *use only approved biological drugs* known by your physician to be free of chemical agents or contaminants and recommended by him. Even though a given synthetic drug may seem to be taken initially without difficulty, if one is already susceptible to many materials of synthetic origin, prolonged use of synthetic chemical drugs often is associated with a spread of susceptibility and an increasing medical problem insofar as susceptibility to the chemical environment is concerned.

Cosmetics. Commercially available lipstick, nail polish, nail polish remover, perfume, cologne, scented soap and shampoo, detergent shampoo, cold cream, foundation cream, deodorants, after-shaving lotion, hair tonic, hair spray, hair oil, hair dye, mouth wash, some dentifrices and denture adhesives, bath salts, pine-scented oils and toilet preparations may cause reactions. *Use only prescribed cosmetics.*

Clothing, Bedding and Personal Contacts. Troublesome reactions may occur from drip-dry and other finishes of cotton and other natural textiles. Although the formaldehyde treatment of cotton may be largely removed by washing, many cotton goods—especially bed linens—usually have a plasticized starch surface treatment which is capable of eliciting troublesome reactions and is not removed by laundering. Recently cleaned clothing, blankets or furs, or the pressing of recently cleaned materials may not be tolerated. DDT is used in some dry cleaning fluids, especially on woolens. Direct contact with detergents or with bedding or clothing washed with detergents, or dried in gas dryers, or treated with disinfectants may cause reactions in susceptible persons. It often is necessary to avoid the use of rubber-containing garters, brassieres, girdles and corsets; electric blankets and other rubber-containing bedding and upholstery; such synthetic textiles as Nylon, Dacron, Orlon and others—especially when these come in direct contact with the skin as in undergarments—nightgowns, sweaters and robes. Although Rayon is the best tolerated synthetic textile and Nylon is next, their finishes may also cause reactions in the highly susceptible. Plastic brushes, combs, purses, powder boxes, plastic upholstered chairs, stools, tables and desks and plastic telephones may also cause symptoms as a result of direct contact. Formica rarely has been incriminated and only in the highly susceptible as a result of prolonged direct contact. Bakelite telephones and other bakelite plastics usually are tolerated.

Miscellaneous. Contact with lubricating oils, liquid fuels, solvents, polishes, waxes, chemicals used in photography, bleaches or heavily chlorinated water in swimming pools may cause reactions. Numerous other chemical exposures have been incriminated, but their essential *occupational nature* precludes their detailed description here.

FOODS COMMONLY CONTAMINATED BY CHEMICALS

1. *Foods often containing spray residues:* a) Apple, cherry, peach, apricot, nectarine, pear, plum, olive, current, persimmon, strawberry, cranberry, raspberry, blueberry, boysenberry, pineapple, rhubarb, grape, orange, grapefruit and lemon. b) Brussel sprouts, broccoli, cauliflower, cabbage, head lettuce, tomato (hot house grown), celery, asparagus, spinach, beet greens, chard, mustard greens, endive, escarole, leaf lettuce, romaine, Chinese cabbage and artichoke. Most currently used sprays of the chlorinated hydrocarbon type are oil soluble and *permeate the food to which they are applied.* They are *not* removed by washing, peeling, soaking in water or vinegar or by cooking. Root vegetables are apt to be free of spray residues unless contaminated in transit or in mar-

kets. c) Lamb, beef, and sometimes pork and fowl may be contaminated by the animals having eaten sprayed forage and concentrating such oil soluble insecticides, herbicides or their vehicles in their *fats*. Chicken and turkey often contain residues of a synthetic hormone—stilbestriol.

2. *Foods often containing fumigant residues:* Dates, figs, shelled nuts, raisins, prunes and other dried fruits; wheat, corn, rye, barley, rice, dried peas, dried beans, lentils.

3. *Foods often containing bleaches:* White flour. Unbleached flour usually is available. Although white flour is often "enriched" with synthetic chemicals, it is still *impoverished*. Freshly ground whole wheat flour is far more nutritious and better tasting.

4. *Foods often treated with sulfur:* Peach, apricot, and nectarine may be dusted with sulfur as a fungicidal agent. Commercially prepared fresh apple, fresh apricot, fresh peach and French fried potato may be treated with sulfur dioxide as an anti-browning agent. Molasses, dried fruit, melon and citrus candied peel and fruit marmalade may be bleached with sulfur dioxide. Dried apple, dried pear, dried peach, dried apricot, raisin, prune, corn syrup (glucose), corn sugar (dextrose), cornstarch and corn oil usually are treated with sulfur dioxide in the process of manufacture.

5. *Foods artificially colored:* Creme de menthe, maraschino cherries and other colored fruit; Jello and other colored gelatin desserts; mint sauce, colored ice cream, colored sherbet, colored candy, colored cake, cookie and pie frostings and fillings; wieners, bologna, cheese, butter, oleomargarine; orange, sweet potato, Irish potato, root beer, pop, cola drinks and certain other soft and imitation drinks usually contain coal-tar dyes.

6. *Foods artificially sweetened:* Any containing saccharine or Sucaryl (sodium cyclomate).

7. *Foods exposed to gas:* Bananas often are artificially ripened by exposure to ethylene gas. Apple and pear are sometimes stored in the presence of ethylene gas. Coffee is usually roasted over an open gas flame and may absorb some of the combustion products of such a flame. Cane and beet sugars usually are clarified by being filtered through bone char. These filters usually are re-activated periodically in gas-fired kilns. Absorbed combustion

products apparently are imparted to the next batch of syrup which is filtered through them. Raw sugar may be somewhat less contaminated. Honey is the preferred sweetening agent.

8. *Foods contaminated by containers:* Carrot, parsnip, turnip, tomato and mixed shredded greens are sometimes dispensed in odorous plastic bags. Certain other foods may also be contaminated by having been transported, stored or frozen in plastic containers. Cellophane wrapped foodstuffs are usually tolerated by chemically susceptible patients. In general, plastic wrappings tend to contaminate their food contents in direct proportion to the odor emitted by the wrapping material. If odorous or if rubbing or filing the surface of a plastic wrapper causes the emission of an odor, there is increased reason for suspecting it. The longer a food remains in an odorous plastic wrapping, the more it may be contaminated. Plastic refrigerator dishes for storage of foods are commonly incriminated. Citrus fruit may be contaminated chemically by fungicide treated containers.

Foods are frequently contaminated by the golden brown lining of metal cans. This lining—most commonly a phenolic resin—prevents the metal from bleaching the can contents but also contaminates them chemically. Only such foods as the manufacturer desires to bleach (asparagus, grapefruit, pineapple, artichoke and some citrus juices) are apt to be packed in unlined tins.

9. *Foods often waxed with paraffin:* Rutabaga, parsnip, turnip, pepper, apple, orange, grapefruit, tangerine and lemon may be waxed and/or polished. Apple, cucumber, eggplant and green pepper may be lightly waxed and polished.

10. *Foods often containing desiccating agents:* Triscuits and prepared cocoanut often contain added glycols.

FOODS THAT USUALLY ARE LESS CHEMICALLY CONTAMINATED

Fish and Meat. Fresh or frozen seafood (lobster, crayfish or lobster tail, shrimp, crab and others), fresh fish or fish which has been frozen in large pieces (in contrast to pound packages) are not usually contaminated. Lean meat from which the fat has been stripped prior to cooking is preferable to cooking meat with its adherent fat.

Vegetables. Fresh potato (if undyed and home peeled), turnip, rutabaga, eggplant, and parsnip (if not waxed), tomato (if field ripened), carrot (if not bagged in odorous plastic), squash, onion, pumpkin, beet, (tops are usually sprayed), salsify, celery root, parsley root, okra, green peas and green beans (if fresh, fresh frozen or canned in glass).

Fruit. Nuts in shell only (Brazil nut, cocoanut, walnut, hickory nut, pecan, filbert, hazelnut).

Sweetening agents. Honey, sorghum and pure maple.

Fats and Oils. Olive, cottonseed, peanut, soy, cocoanut, sunflower, sesame, safflower, preferably *cold pressed* rather than extracted by the usual solvent processes. Buckwheat.

Importations such as chocolate, arrowroot, tapioca, carob and sassafras tea usually have been fumigated in shiphold.

Any food may have been contaminated in transit or in markets by sprayed surroundings in contaminated bulk cartons, plastic bags or DDT-treated burlap bags.

Uncontaminated Food Sources. Foods from approved local sources should be secured for canning in glass or freezing in glass or aluminum foil during the season of availability.

Membership in State and local Natural Food Associates groups or Organic Gardening Clubs is helpful in finding sources of supply.

Discussion and Summary

Most persons remain adapted to the conditions of their existence without becoming specifically susceptible to various environmental substances and without manifesting ill health from exposure to them. Of those who do become susceptible to one or more environmental materials, including items of the diet, many remain specifically adapted for long periods without obvious ill effects. Sooner or later, however, adaptation tends to taper off and chronic symptoms ensue. Although this may involve a single excitant, susceptibility and maladaptation to multiple environmental exposures is the rule. Under such circumstances, the common causes of chronic ills are rarely suspected.

The range of manifestations encompasses localized and constitutional reactions as well as physical and mental syndromes, including an alternating relationship between levels and phases of chronic and acute effects. The clinical picture presented at any given time depends principally on factors of specific exposure, susceptibility and adaptation in the sense of the body's over-all defenses.

The three major causes of reactions on the basis of individual susceptibility and exposure to environmental materials are: 1) Inhaled particles (pollens, dusts, molds, danders, et cetera); 2) Foods, and 3) Chemical additives and contaminants of air, food, water, biological drugs and chemical drugs, as well as perfumes, cosmetics, and certain other man-made synthetic materials referred to as the *chemical environment.*

Individual susceptibility to the chemical environment or parts of it must be carefully differentiated from the *clinical effects resulting from other environmental excitants* with which it usually coexists. For instance, susceptibility to chemical additives and contaminants of the food supply must be separated from food susceptibility *per se.* Indeed, susceptibility to all three groups of environmental excitants is to be expected until *demonstrated not to exist.* Likewise, susceptibility to one or more potential excitants is not to be assumed until *demonstrated to exist.*

Because of the *unreliability of individual histories,* both of these tasks are facilitated by a program of comprehensive environmental control in which the most probable excitants are avoided concurrently. After chronic effects resulting from oft-repeated exposures have subsided, isolated re-exposures to which high degrees of susceptibility exist then induce acute reactions which demonstrate *cause and effect. Treatment consists of avoiding incriminating excitants,* thereby decreasing the load of materials to which adaptation is being attempted.

In contrast to naturally occurring relatively inert physical and biological substances capable of inducing specific susceptibility and manifesting as chronic illness, the *man-made chemical environment* is both more recent and more reactive.

Although many seem to be adapting satisfactorily to these new living conditions, susceptibility to one or more facets of the chemical environment apparently is increasing as the totality of such exposures accumulate. It would appear only a matter of time before many of those apparently adapting satisfactorily to one or more of these exposures succumb to the oft-repeated thrusts of a given facet of the chemical environment. Once such a maladaptation has occurred, susceptibility not only tends to *increase in degree* but appears to *spread* to related materials to which frequent exposures also occur. Chronic illness ensues as adaptive abilities wear down. Whereas at first these changes occurred principally in the elderly and the young, they are now becoming increasingly common in middle age as well as during reproductive and adolescent years.

Despite the rapidly increasing knowledge of the chemical make-up of the world and the ability of the human race to construct a *chemical environment, man remains a biologic phenomenon.* Individual man adapts or fails to adapt to the circumstances of his existence, as does any other living thing. Despite our rapidly increasing knowledge of the chemical basis of physiology, we are unable, as yet, to avoid the development of such maladapted states associated with chronic symptom syndromes or to reverse the course of this process, once it has developed.

One cannot escape the deduction that susceptibility to and maladaptation to the chemical environment and illnesses associated therewith are early manifestations of degeneration. Whatever it may be called, one thing is certain: individuals who become highly susceptible and maladapted to one or more common chemical excitants are usually *not the same thereafter.* Although many may be maintained symptom-free in a controlled or more primitive existence, such avoidance programs are becoming increasingly difficult to maintain, due to the increasing ubiquity of chemical surroundings. Moreover, a symptom-free state may also be precluded by the common coexistence of individual susceptibility to various physical and biological exposures which are also impossible to avoid.

However, the general rule that *finding and avoiding causes of illness is better than treating the effects of illness* still holds. Despite the restrictive nature of the therapeutic program, the outlook for the chemically susceptible person is far less bleak than may be inferred from the above generalizations. First of all, no person is susceptible to *all* the facets of the chemical environment. Many times the relatively few chemical excitants impinging on a patient may be easily avoided. Secondly, if the degree of susceptibility is not excessive, avoidance of massive doses may be sufficient to relieve symptoms. Such a person may then be able to adapt satisfactorily to lesser doses which cannot be avoided as readily. Lastly, it is a great source of satisfaction to a chronically ill person to know *why* he is sick—even though a completely satisfactory solution to his problem may not be available as a result of avoiding incriminated causes. At least, having a specific diagnosis and attempting to avoid incriminated excitants tends to break the everlasting continuity of undiagnosed chronic illness resulting from daily exposures. Although acute reactions arising from *accidental exposures* may be temporarily more severe than the previous level of chronic symptoms, such acute responses are ordinarily of relatively short duration and may be treated much more effectively. Moreover, acute reactions of *known causation* are infinitely more endurable than chronic illness of *unknown origin*.

The more commonly pursued alternative of treating the effects of chronic illness without demonstrating its causes may be especially hazardous for the chemically susceptible person. When already susceptible and reacting to one or more chemical excitants, the use of *additional* synthetically derived chemical drugs is neither sound nor effective. Under such circumstances, superimposed acute or chronic reactions are to be expected, in view of the ease with which susceptibility tends to spread to materials of common genesis. All too frequently, such a course adds to the victim's total burden by complicating or perpetuating his illness.

This presentation purposely has emphasized the *totality of the chemical environment* to which the most highly susceptible person may react, for two reasons: 1) This is an effective teaching method, for once the total scope and extreme manifestations of a clinical problem are grasped, more commonly occurring but lesser degrees of the same problem tend to be more apparent. 2) This is more practical as compared with the way this subject has ordinarily been presented. This orientation, stressing *multiple reactions of a single person,* is more helpful to the practitioner sitting across from a sick patient than a knowledge of the *statistical incidence of reactions* to certain chemical compounds occurring in a *large group of subjects.*

In summary: This presentation deals with MAN as a *biological unit* and his *adaptation to a chemically contaminated world.*

REFERENCES

1. Haeckel, E.: *Generelle Morphologie der Organismen*, Berlin, G. Reimer, 1866.

2. Darwin, C. R.: *On the Origin of Species by Means of Natural Selection*, New York, D. Appleton & Co., 1860.

3. Randolph, T. G. and Mitchell, D. S.: Specific Ecology and Chronic Illness, *J. Lab. & Clin. Med.*, 52:936-937, 1958.

4. Randolph, T. G.: The Planned Maneuver of the Patient—A Third Dimension of the Medical Investigation, Clinical Physiology, *Clin. Physiol.*, 2:42-47, 1960.

5. Randolph, T. G.: Sensitivity to Pine, Petroleum, Coal-tar and Derivatives, Ninth Ann. Cong. Amer. Coll. Allergists, Chicago, 1953.

6. Randolph, T. G.: Allergic-type Reactions to Industrial Solvents and Liquid Fuels; Mosquito Abatement Fogs and Mists; Motor Exhausts; Indoor Utility Gas and Oil Fumes; Chemical Additives of Foods and Drugs; and, Synthetic Drugs and Cosmetics, *J. Lab. & Clin. Med.*, 44:910-914, 1954.

7. Randolph, T. G.: Depressions Caused by Home Exposures to Gas and Combustion Products of Gas, Oil and Coal, *J. Lab. & Clin. Med.*, 46: 942, 1955.

8. Randolph, T. G.: Food Susceptibility (Food Allergy), *Current Therapy*, Philadelphia, Saunders, 1960, pp. 418-423.

9. Selye, H.: The General Adaptation Syndrome and the Diseases of Adaptation, *J. Allergy*, 17:231, 289, 358, 1946.

10. Selye, H.: *Stress*, Montreal, Acta, Inc., 1950.

11. Adolph, E. F.: General and Specific Characteristics of Physiological Adaptations, *Amer. J. Physiol.*, 184:18-28, 1956.

12. Randolph, T. G.: The Specific Adaptation Syndrome, *J. Lab. & Clin. Med., 48:*934, 1956.

13. Rinkel, H. J., Randolph, T. G. and Zeller, M.: *Food Allergy,* Springfield, Thomas, 1950.

14. Savage, G. H.: *Insanity and Allied Neuroses,* Phila., Henry C. Lea's Son & Co., 1884.

15. Randolph, T. G.: The Alternation of the Symptoms of Allergy and Those of Alcoholism and Certain Mental Disturbances, *J. Lab. & Clin. Med., 40:*932, 1952.

16. Randolph, T. G.: The Descriptive Features of Food Addiction; Addictive Eating and Drinking, *Quart. Rev. of Studies on Alcohol, 17:*198-224, 1956.

17. Randolph, T. G.: Ecologic Mental Illness—Psychiatry Exteriorized. *J. Lab. & Clin. Med., 54:*936, 1959.

18. Randolph, T. G.: An Ecologic Orientation in Medicine, submitted for publication.

19. Brown, E. A. and Colombo, N. J.: The Asthmathogenic Effects of Odors, Smells and Fumes, *Ann. Allergy, 12:*14-24, 1954.

20. Brown, E. A.: Persistent Cough and Bronchospasm Due to Exposure to Fumes from Range Oil; A New Clinical Syndrome. *Ann. Allergy, 7:*756-760, 1949.

21. Coca, A. F.: *Familial Non-reaginic Food Allergy,* Springfield, Thomas (3rd ed.) 1953.

22. Duke, W. W.: *Allergy; Asthma, Hay Fever, Urticaria and Allied Manifestations of Reaction,* St. Louis, Mosby (2nd ed.) 1926.

23. Rowe, A. H.: *Clinical Allergy,* Phila., Lea and Febiger, 1937.

24. Coca, A. F.: *Familial Non-reaginic Food Allergy,* Springfield, Thomas, (2nd ed.) 1945.

25. Urbach, E. and Gottlieb, P. M.: New York, Grune & Stratton, 1943.

26. Wittich, F. W.: Respiratory Tract Allergic Effects from Chemical Air Pollution, *Arch. Ind. Hygiene and Occup. Med., 2:*329, 1950.

27. Vaughan, W. T.: *Practice of Allergy*, St. Louis, C. V. Mosby, 1939.

28. Follansbee, Rogers: personal communication.

29. Knight, Granville: personal communication.

30. Gardner, H. G.: Allergy and Industry, *Ann. Allergy, 10:*732-744, 1952.

31. Netherlands Society of Allergy: *Occupational Allergy*, Springfield, Thomas, 1958.

32. Rowe, A. H., Rowe, A. Jr., and Young, E. J.: Bronchial Asthma Due to Food Allergy Alone in 95 Patients, *J.A.M.A., 169:*1158-1162, 1959.

33. Randolph, T. G.: Chemical Contaminants of Foods, 19th Series of the Letters of the International Correspondence Society of Allergists, p. 5; Editor—Jonathan Forman, Dublin, Ohio.

34. Randolph, T. G. and Rollins, J. P.: Allergic Reactions from the Ingestion of Intravenous Injection of Cane Sugar (Sucrose), *J. Lab. & Clin. Med., 36:*242-248, 1950.

35. Lee, R.: Plastics in Your Food, *Lets Live, 27:*8, 1959.

36. Watson, S. H. and Kibler, C. S.: Drinking Water as Cause of Asthma, *J. Allergy, 5:*197, 1934.

37. Schroeder, H. A.: Relation between Mortality from Cardiovascular Disease and Treated Water Supplies, *J.A.M.A., 172:* 1902-1908, 1960.

38. Glaser, J.: *Allergy in Childhood*, Springfield, Thomas, 1956.

39. Randolph, T. G.: Allergy to So-called "Inert Ingredients" (Excipients) of Pharmaceutical Preparations, *Ann. Allergy, 8:*519-529, 1950.

40. Hubata, J. A., Medical Director, Amour Pharmaceutical Company, Chicago, Ill., Personal Communication.

41. Pfeiffer, E. E.: A Quantitative Chromatographic Method for the Determination of Biological Factors, Bio-Dynamics, Bio-Dynamic Farming and Gardening Assn., Inc., Dover Plains, N. Y., Spring 1959, pp. 2-15.

42. Schwartz, L.; Tulipan, L.; and Birmingham, D. J.: *Occupational Diseases of the Skin*, Phila., Lea & Febiger, 3rd Ed., 1957.

43. Mitchell, E. S., Drummond Medical Bldg., Montreal Que. Canada,: Personal Communication.

44. Clark, H. G. and Randolph, T. G.: The Acid-Anoxia-Endocrine Theory of Allergy, *J. Lab. & Clin. Med., 36*:811-812, 1950.

45. Randolph, T. G. and Clark, H. G.: Sodium Bicarbonate in the Treatment of Allergic Conditions, *J. Lab. & Clin. Med., 44*: 915, 1954.

46. Godlowski, Z. Z.: Endocrine Management of Selected Cases of Allergy Based on Enzymatic Mechanism of Sensitization, *A.M.A. Arch. Otolar., 7*:515-557, 1960.

47. Randolph, T. G. and Clark, H. G.: Discussion of Observations on the Metabolic Changes Resulting from the Administration of ACTH to Patients with Asthma and Allied Conditions, by Rose, B.; Pare, J. A. P.; Pump, K. K.; Sanford, R. L.; Mackenzie, K. R. and Venning, E. H. — *Proc. of the Second Clinical ACTH Conference*, Vol. 1 — Research, pp. 525-527, New York, Blakiston, 1951.

48. Singer, R. B.; Clark, J. K.; Barker, E. S.; Crosley, A. P. Jr., and Elkingon, J. R.: The Acute Effects in Man of Rapid Intravenous Infusion of Hypertonic Sodium Bicarbonate Solution, *Medicine, 34*:51-95, 1955.

49. Randolph, T. G. and Rollins, J. P.: Adrenocorticotropic Hormone (ACTH); Its Effect in Atopic Dermatitis, *Ann. Allergy, 9*:1-10, 1951.

INDEX

Privine, 87
Probability, 91, 108, 118
Procaine, 17, 18, 20
Proneness to reaction, 85
Propane, 56
Prophylaxis, 98, 99
Propinquity, 23
Proprioception, 59
Prosthetic devices, 90
Prune, 30, 115
Pruritus, 12, 21
Psychiatry, 100
Psychoses, 22
Public places, 38, 49, 50, 110
Pulse rate, 19, 33
Pumpkin, 117
Purses, 90
Pyrethrum, 110

Q
Questionnaire, 24, 25
    interpretation of, 31, 32
    rechecking, 37

R
Radio, 49
Rags, greasy, 26, 62
Railroad, sprayed right of ways, 62
    stations, 55
Railroads, 52, 54, 111
Rain, 51
Raisin, 30, 115
Range, kitchen (*see* Gas kitchen range)
Rash, 16
Raspberry, 30, 114
Rayon, 27, 88, 114
Reactions, acute, 5, 23, 34, 35, 36, 49, 54,
    55, 59, 62, 65, 71, 94, 105, 118, 120
    acute, treatment of, 92
    addiction-like, 83
    chronic, 5, 32, 49, 59, 67, 98, 118, 120
    chronic, treatment of, 95
    constitutional, 56, 82
    convincing, 33
    delayed, 22, 36
    depths of, 22, 34
    diagnostic, 22
    drunk-like, 59
    duration of, 120

from air pollution, 101
from drugs, 96
immediate, 22, 35, 36
impaired ability to drive in, 57
incidence of, 121
inhalant, 90
levels of, 22, 23, 118
localized, 56, 82
merging stages, 22, 59
motor phases of, 22
multiplicity of, 95, 120
phases of, 118
proneness to, 85
rapidly advancing, 23
severity of, 65, 72
stimulatory effects of, 33
toxic, 34
treatment of, 34
underestimation of degree, 59
unsuspected, 39
Reading comprehension, 21, 101, 104
Redness of face, 17
Reexposures, 22
Refineries, 20, 35, 51, 52, 111, 112
Refinery fumes, 12
Reflexes, 19
Refrigerants, 44
Refrigerators, 44, 74, 110
    electric, 47
    enamel lined, 14, 75
    plastic lined, 14, 74, 116
    storage, in glass, 14
    storage in plastic, 14
Refuse, burning of, 112
Registers, 40
Regression, 22
Regulations, mandatory, 69
Renal failure, 93
Residues, chemical, 20
Resins, 27, 51, 76
    phenolic, 116
Respiratory symptoms, 21
Response, addiction-like, 4
    clinical, 1
    general pattern of, 24
    individuality of, 24
Responsiveness, 19
Restaurants, 49
Restlessness, 46, 101, 102

DATE DUE

SEP 0 5 1996			
SEP 0 5 1998			
SEP 0 5 1991			